"With *Making Magic*, Briana Saussy provides a clear, welcoming guide to accessing your magic and creating a spiritual path that is all your own. She teaches you to recognize and locate the magical powers that already exist all around you and within you. If that wasn't enough (and really it is), if you, like me, are a fairytale lover, this book contains one of the best versions of Goldilocks ever. Recommended!"

JUDIKA ILLES
author of the *Encyclopedia of 5,000 Spells,*
The Big Book of Practical Spells,
and other books devoted to the magical arts

"This extraordinary little book is the medicine we need now! Many elders say that the global change we need most will come when we make changes inside our own homes. With ourselves. In our families. *Making Magic* instructs you how to begin to walk in your life in a sacred way. I can't wait to share this book and its profoundly beautiful practices with my students!"   SARAH BAMFORD SEIDELMANN
shamanic healer and life coach, author of
The Book of Beasties and *Swimming with Elephants*

"Put down everything you've been told about magic—that it's arcane, occult, and forgotten in the mists of time. Then pick up *Making Magic*. Here you will discover that magic is alive. She is fresh and new, fluid and flexible, and a totally natural and normal part of an everyday life— your everyday life. And the best part? You will remember that the magician is you."   JANET CONNER
author of *Writing Down Your Soul*, creator and host
of the *Praying at the Speed of Love* podcast

"*Making Magic* is a wonderful walk through a world that makes every-thing seem a bit brighter; a shimmer suddenly catches our hearts and minds where before there was darkness. Briana Saussy teaches what magick can be in our lives—an undercurrent of joy at the smallest of occurrences, or the rush when we realize our unlimited potential in cre-ating our own kingdom right here on earth."   DAMIEN ECHOLS
New York Times bestselling author
of *Life After Death* and *High Magick*

"This is a book for those seekers who wish to remember and recover their magic. Briana's wise words and simple rituals make magic accessible to everybody. If you use the practices in this book, you will bring the sacred into your everyday life and find the mystical in the typical. For those who are ready to begin living a magical life, this is the book you've been waiting for."

THERESA REED
author of *The Tarot Coloring Book*

"*Making Magic* is not only the most beautifully written book on any such subject that I have ever read . . . . It's contemporary, erudite, and invigorating yet reassuring."

MYSTIC MEDUSA
writer and astrologer at MysticMedusa.com

"In *Making Magic*, Briana Saussy gets us to the root of magic. She sets aside the arcane ceremonies, ancient chants, and dogmatic rules, and reveals how to weave spells that speak to who you are and the world you are living in. [Y]ou'll feel as if you've been taken under the wing of a loving aunt who is sharing family wisdom with a good dose of humor and common sense. Following the exercises at the end of every chapter will change your life for the better, beyond any shadow of a doubt."

JASON MILLER
author of *Protection and Reversal Magick*,
the *Strategic Sorcery Course*,
and other books and courses

"Briana Saussy truly understands magic: the history, practice, myths, and tales of humankind's age-old relationship with the more-than-human world. In this wise and beautifully crafted book, she guides us through practices designed to open us up to a numinous world that's all around us, at the edge of sight, and to help us live our everyday lives in a mythic, soulful, purposeful way. I have long been a fan of Briana Saussy's work. *Making Magic* is the book I've been waiting for."

TERRI WINDLING
folklorist and author of *The Wood Wife*

"*Making Magic* is a no-nonsense guide to practical magic—meaning magic that changes stuff, ourselves included! Filled with exercises, hands-on work, and guided journaling, it helps us to remember and reimagine what magic can and does mean for each of us. Briana has created a great guide for finding the magic in the world we already inhabit, as well as how to grow it into a stronger, more helpful ally. . . . Highly recommended for those looking for a straightforward and gentle start in the sacred arts, without the necessity of taking on a new faith or tradition or having to learn a lot of occultist jargon."

AIDAN WACHTER
author of *Six Ways: Approaches &*
Entries for Practical Magic

"In a sea of seemingly endless treatises on magic, Briana's work is absolutely unique. The means by which she weaves ritual construction, magical theory, and useful, no-nonsense exercises into such an eloquent, cohesive, functional system of sorcery is both poetic and pragmatic. *Making Magic* is a blessing—a means by which you can genuinely improve and enrich your life and the lives of those around you . . . [A] tremendously important, absolutely ground-breaking work."   **ELIZABETH BARRIAL**
perfumer-in-chief for Black Phoenix Alchemy Lab

"Rich with mythology and dripping in the sweet honey of folklore, this book will lift your ordinary days into the extraordinary, with gratitude for the mystery and opportunity for ritual that surrounds you."

PIXIE LIGHTHORSE
author of *Prayers of Honoring*

"In *Making Magic*, you won't find demands to seek high and low for esoteric supplies, or confusing references that obfuscate rather than clarify. Saussy's book is a beautifully grounded resource about the magic we can make in our everyday lives, weaving sacred practice into the fabric of our very spirits."   **ESMÉ WEIJUN WANG**
author of *The Border of Paradise*
and *The Collected Schizophrenias*

"From the first paragraph, I was enchanted by *Making Magic*. . . . Let Briana Saussy help you remember all you once knew: that your holy helpers have your back, that the herbs and spices on your kitchen shelf hold potent magic, that sending out a call means there will be a response. You only need to hone the skill to recognize it. And this book will show you how. *Making Magic* is a precious touchstone—just right for beginners on the path, as well as more seasoned soulful seekers."

JOANNA POWELL COLBERT
creator of the *Gaian Tarot* and
co-creator of the *Herbcrafter's Tarot*

"This book is a must read for anyone interested in learning how to wake up in an exciting and mystical way. . . . Through her beautiful writing, Briana Saussy takes the reader on an adventure to deepen one's soul. She uses a mixture of poetic imagery and guided steps to help people find their own magic and what makes them feel alive."

JOHN LOCKLEY
author of *Leopard Warrior*

"One of my favorite things about Briana Saussy is the way she encourages people to find their own way and make their own meaning. She'll give you guidelines and suggestions, but the real magic is in listening to your own heart, opening and deepening a relationship with the numinous life inside and around you. Let Briana be your guide to your own magic."

MEGAN DEVINE
author of *It's OK That You're Not OK*

"This book is a zephyr—a playful breeze that rustles the veil separating the ordinary from the magical, revealing a landscape wherein every particle of being shimmers with the sacred. This holy ground, as it turns out, is where we already live. We need only pay attention, and claim it, and praise it."

MIRABAI STARR
author of *God of Love* and
Caravan of No Despair

BRIANA SAUSSY

Weaving Together the Everyday and the Extraordinary

sounds true
BOULDER, COLORADO

Sounds True
Boulder, CO 80306

Published 2019

Cover design by Lisa Kerans
Book design by Beth Skelley

Cover and interior illustrations by Cassandra Oswald

Printed in Canada

Library of Congress Cataloging-in-Publication Data
Names: Saussy, Briana, author.
Title: Making magic : weaving together the everyday and the
    extraordinary / Briana H. Saussy.
Description: Boulder : Sounds True, 2019. | Includes bibliographical
    references.
Identifiers: LCCN 2018041616 (print) | LCCN 2018047736 (ebook) |
    ISBN 9781683643371 (ebook) | ISBN 9781683642480 (pbk.)
Subjects: LCSH: Magic.
Classification: LCC BF1611 (ebook) | LCC BF1611 .S28 2019 (print) |
    DDC 133.4/3—dc23
LC record available at https://lccn.loc.gov/2018041616

10 9 8 7 6 5 4 3 2 1

To the ones who came before and whose voices were not heard.

For my sons, Jasper and Heath, and all who will come after.

And in deepest gratitude and love to those who hold me now:
my parents, sister, and grandmother.

Above all, to my best beloved, David, who fills my life with magic.

With an eye made quiet by the power
of harmony, and the deep power of joy,
we see into the life of things.

WILLIAM WORDSWORTH
"Lines Composed a Few Miles Above Tintern Abbey"

CONTENTS

PRELUDE

Somewhere in the world right now there is a young man collecting railroad spikes. He is walking the tracks while the sun rises, picking up the big iron nails that are pulled up and cast aside by the force of the speeding trains. Once he has enough, he will take them back to his newly purchased property, sink them into the soft earth, magically nailing down his home and land and protecting all who dwell upon it with the strength of iron.

Somewhere in the world right now a woman kneels down as she strikes a match, lights a candle, closes her eyes, and recites a blessing for her beloveds. After rising up on creaky knees, she kisses the face of her favored holy helper, offering up a tin *milagro* tied to a bright ribbon as a gesture of thanksgiving. She is not alone, for there are many others, speaking to their chosen saints, angels, and holy helpers too.

Somewhere in the world right now a child is recounting her dream, while a grown-up listens, helping her make sense of it and asking her of the ways that the dream world speaks to the world here and now.

Somewhere in the world right now a couple about to wed sits down together. They eat figs and dates, drink champagne, and laughingly fill a clear crystal jar with layers of golden honey, red and pink rose petals, and orange flowers, before topping it off with a bit of hot cinnamon, so that their relationship will always be sweet, their marriage blessed, and their lovemaking spicy.

Somewhere in the world right now a mother prepares a sacred bath for her son who is moving into puberty. She adds roots and flowers, leaves and stems, oils and salts, so that her child is protected and safe as he navigates the ever more intense labyrinth that is young male adulthood.

Somewhere in the world right now a soon-to-be father sees his partner struggling in the early pains of labor and draws an old knife out of his pocket, placing it under the birthing bed, so that its honed edge can cut the pain of labor as easily as it cuts through butter.

Somewhere in the world right now people are building their altars, making offerings, praying down hard, and discovering the power of the extraordinary in a thousand unique ways. They are not priestesses in remote mountains or shamans in hard-to-find villages. They are ordinary people with families, jobs, worries, and loves, just like you and just like me. They are men and women, old ones and young ones, creating better, deeper lives.

Somewhere in the world right now there are people from every conceivable culture, walk of life, and set of experiences who all have one thing in common: they have remembered. They are making magic.

Are you ready to make it too?

INTRODUCTION

Children recognize magic at first sight. One day when I was about eleven years old, while wandering in the woods near my house, I found Licorice's body. Licorice had been a sleek, short-haired tomcat, white and blacker than licorice, black like the night far away from cities. He was one of my favorite childhood cats among several who roamed far and wide, all shrewd and competent mousers. We all noticed he had been gone for weeks, and nobody knew where he was. We assumed that eventually he'd return in his own time, as is the way with cats.

I stayed with Licorice for a long time. His body was already in an advanced state of decay and partially covered by earth. Parts of his delicate white skeleton were exposed and already bleached by the South Texas sun. When I found him, I knew I needed to mark the event of his death in some manner. He needed a memorial.

The first thing I did was prepare a grave, dug far enough into a patch of earth that his body would not be easily found by wild animals. I then set to the task of taking care of his body, picking him up and washing him down. I gathered some fresh lavender from the bush where he liked to sleep, and I placed the lavender with his body before I shrouded it. After I buried him in the earth, I sang over him. I don't remember what I sang, but I do know that it was a healing song and my gift to Licorice.

The whole process was as natural as taking a deep breath. I was not trying to prove how outlandish I could be or how rebellious I was. I was just sharing something straight from the heart, from my little being to his and to the land.

The death and ritual burial of Licorice, while one little girl's experience, points the way to a possibility confirmed by many people in countless ways, according to their own intimate experiences. We all have a deep capacity to make magic and to do it as easily as we breathe or open our eyes. This is not a matter of belief. You can discover your capacity for magic through your own direct experience. Recognizing it, then, is simply a matter of sufficient attention, memory, and reflection on experience. What we finally choose to do with this human capacity for magic will look different for everyone, but the very capacity for it flows from a human experience that is at once profoundly personal and intimate, and universal and open to all.

The million-dollar question is, what are we looking for when we make magic?

As it happens, I am in a unique position to answer this question. That little girl who reframed and thereby transformed a painful event with a series of simple, loving gestures—such as singing, cleansing, and placing carefully chosen flowers—grew into womanhood and became a teacher, writer, diviner, ritualist, and practitioner of the sacred arts. What I see in my work with people of many walks of life, listening to the stories they tell me about their own lives, is this: we are all looking for a way to heal the deepest rifts and fractures of life. The most beautiful, the most magical, of all things we can do is to find the means to reframe and unify the deepest discords not only within ourselves but also in our relationships—with other people, with animals, and with our world—to heal our broken planet. I have also found that the greatest rift of all is the one that cuts apart the everyday from the extraordinary.

There are many ways to go about doing the work of healing, of reconciliation and unification, of seeking and making something of our findings. Making magic, weaving together the everyday and the extraordinary, is one of those ways.

You will find that this book on magic presents a very different view from others. There are no occult or arcane systems, no rigid sets of symbolic correspondences to memorize, no elaborate ceremonial rituals to perform hailing from the Victorian era and largely created by men. Instead, you will discover a series of indications and directions you can explore yourself. For what we need most in our soulful seeking is to learn how to create rituals and ceremonies that are both meaningful to us and relevant to our immediate lives.

My approach to magic is grounded in and draws from multiple cultural traditions, as does my own lineage, and I have also been blessed to work with clients and students from around the world, many of whom have shared with me their own cultural traditions and the little acts of everyday life that are spilling over with magic. This unique vantage point, combined with my own cultural and educational background, has allowed me to sift through the tales I have heard and the traditions, spells, charms, rites, and ceremonies I have encountered to get down to the foundation of why people seek out magic. What I have discovered is that it always comes down to choice—a choice that needs to be made. This is the real gift of magic: it reveals possibilities and potentials that were previously thought to be unreal or impossible. In short, while we seek out magic for many reasons, chief among them is the fact that it restores our sense of sovereignty. I want you to be able to remember the roots of magic for yourself, from the basis of your own experience, so that you can create magic in just the way that makes sense for your life and beliefs.

The structure of this book is simple, with a view of magic that is practical both in terms of approach and results. Instead of organizing chapters by desired end goals (such as love, sex, and relationships; health and healing; money and prosperity), I am taking a more unconventional approach and organizing the chapters by techniques and materials. In this way, we cover areas like gardening, cooking, bathing, lighting candles, and so on. This approach gives us a more natural entry point into our own experience of magic.

Though you may never have been interested in or encountered magic on your own, you will no doubt have trafficked with some of its relatives, perhaps without realizing it. The practice of magic, like each of us, does not live in a vacuum but rather is part of a vibrant community, a family that I call the sacred arts. These interrelated practices have been part of the human experience and human story since there have been people to practice them. The sacred arts include:

- right relationship

- magic and alchemy

- prayer, meditation, and blessing

- ceremony and ritual

- lineage and legacy

- divination, astrology, and dreams

- purification and cleansing

The sacred arts listed above do not compose a rational system; they are simply a description of practices that human beings participate in all over the world. Typically, these practices are taken separately, in isolation from one another, and the whole is forgotten. Some of these practices, like magic, have been hidden, covered over, and burned out over the centuries, condemned and outlawed by big religions and even bigger modern authorities. Yet they, like wild creatures, have endured. As we remember our magic, seek it out, and discover anew the extraordinary within the everyday, we will touch upon all of the sacred arts. We cannot touch one without touching all. By seeing magic as part of a vibrant whole, you will gain creative access to the deepest sources of the whole-making power that is yours and yours alone.

This has been my experience of the sacred arts, and it is why I have chosen to dedicate my life and work to sharing them with my community of soulful seekers. Magic has always been my personal entryway into this world. Born with a cleft palate, amid a herd of doctors doubtful of my ability to survive, I was a creature of two worlds early on. There was the world of here and now, the everyday, and the world where the stories came from and the faeries lived—the extraordinary. I was fortunate to be nourished by a steady diet of medicine stories and by a clan of people who are in their own ways as wild as magic itself. Taught from an early age about prayer, divination, and ritual, I took to magic with ease and spent my afternoons instructing a rapt audience of stuffed animals about the finer points of spell craft. As I grew older, I discovered that not everyone shared my mystical bent, and at the same time, I saw that those who were drawn to magic often meant something quite different by the term than I did. The little tricks, medicines, and routines that I had been given in subtle, often quite casual ways had never been called magic. It was just the stuff my family did, the way we lived.

As I augmented my early education with more formal training in magic and a college education in classics from both the

Western and Eastern traditions, I began to understand that what I knew to be magic and the sacred arts have always been with us but rarely spied in their natural habitats and seldom witnessed within their pack. Throughout my college years, I would cast natal charts and divine for my friends, but it never occurred to me that the cap of professional sacred artist and magic maker was the one I was called to wear. In truth, the transition happened so naturally that I barely saw it. Friends came for counsel through divination and astrology. My counsel led to suggestions of rituals to try and magic to make, and my friends became clients, who in turn referred others to me. Slowly a community of bright and brilliant people, who I refer to as *soulful seekers*, began to grow around me. When I look back, I see that the roads were all leading to this point, and I feel deeply grateful and privileged every day that I am able to do this work, surrounded by such a beautiful community.

And as I have engaged in this work, I have learned so very much more about magic. Everyone I speak to and work with comes to the table already knowing deep down what they need or want, but they do not always have the right language with which to frame or articulate those knowings. Finding this language is a deeply personal and profound process that requires effort and speaks directly to our practical needs. The person who knows how to make magic intuitively grasps how to create a ritual to honor a damaged relationship with a family member, understands why she might choose this outfit over another when she goes in to close the big deal, and is able to create the "just right" ceremony to honor a beloved who has died and now needs to be remembered. And here's the big secret: you know too.

Our journey through this book begins with an overview of magic and a consideration of what its native terrain might look like. We will consider some of the ways that magic has been presented and thought about that are not quite accurate or complete, and we will begin to intentionally track the magic that is already present in our lives. From there, we are going to wander and wonder at how some of the most everyday experiences—going in and out of doors, collecting seemingly random objects, scheduling our time, making and maintaining friendships, experiencing the natural world, and tending to our homes—are all areas ripe and bursting with magic. We will uncover how simple acts like sleeping, dreaming, speaking, bathing, and lighting candles speak directly to a great sense of mystery and possibility. As we explore this terrain together, we will see how even things as fundamental as the clothes in our closets and the bowls in our kitchen cabinets hold magic in their very fibers and contours. While some might criticize this approach as a way of saying that all things are magical so therefore nothing is magical, what we will discover is that magic actually permeates our everyday lives, and the more places we know to look for it, the better able we are to start anywhere, to start with what feels just right to us.

And as it happens, there is a story about that.

GOLDEN LOCKS AND THE BEAR PEOPLE

Once upon a time, in the place where your home sits now, there was a young girl who lived in a small village that sat on the outskirts of the wild woods. When she was born, the girl's mother wove a beautiful headband for her. It was made of silk and lace and was the color of the golden sun pouring out over honey and of the bright yellow harvest moon and of the candles that flickered in the deep night when the snowy winds howled. This woven headband of silk and lace earned the girl the nickname Golden Locks, and so she was known throughout the village.

It was not allowed for young children, especially young girls, to go into the woods by themselves, for the villagers all swore that the animals in this forest were keenly intelligent and tricky, and liked nothing better than to devour sweet and tender little children. But this young girl kept dreaming about the forest and those who lived within it, especially the Bear People. Finally, after the third night of dreaming, she woke up as the sun began to crest the treetops and knew that today she would go into the woods because, as her dreams had told her, the Bear People still knew about magic, and she wanted them to teach her.

The morning widened and deepened its reach into the day, and the young girl put on her best deerskin shoes and her finest dress, embroidered with roses and beads and birds. She took a clay pot full of honey down from the kitchen shelf so that she might take a worthy offering to the Bear People, for it was known that they deeply loved the magic that the Bee People made.

And so, she set off walking, one foot in front of the other, into the woods. She continued walking throughout the day, until night found Golden Locks cold, hungry, and tired. Finding herself in a little clearing, under the stars and the light of a crescent moon, yet still surrounded by the deep dark woods, she felt the first stirring of doubt within her breast. Was she crazy? Was this a fool's errand? Perhaps she would be devoured by the Bear People or lose her way back out of the forest and never see her family again. But she remembered her dreams and said to herself in a fierce whisper, "I will find magic."

She continued walking, now with the heavenly lights blazing in her heart, and she soon discovered a stony cave hidden by moss and lichen and great trees. Golden Locks knew at once that this was the place where the Bear People could be found. There was a great river rushing through the land, separating where she stood from the cave. She knew that the cave that belonged to the Bear People could move with ease from one part of the forest to another, for it was as magical as they were. If that happened, she might never find it again. So, though she was colder, hungrier, and even more exhausted than she had been, she tied up her skirts and plunged into the icy waters. Instantly she woke up, came to her senses, and swam strong until she reached the other side of the river.

Approaching the entrance to the cave, she saw that it was swept clean, and she could feel the delicious warmth of the Bear People's breath on her night-chilled skin. She paused at the cave's entrance, bowed in the way of her people, and offered up the sweet honey. Within the cave, three pairs of eyes blinked at her curiously. One pair belonged to the largest of the bears, battle-scarred Father Bear, who had sharp and strong teeth. Another set of curious eyes belonged to a smaller bear, who had lighter fur and swollen teats oozing milk—watchful Mother Bear. The final pair of sleepy eyes gazed out at Golden Locks from the face of the smallest bear, who was just about the same size as she and had already stuck his paw into the honey jar, licking it happily with his long, pink tongue. Here, then, was Baby Bear.

Baby Bear met Golden Locks' eyes with his own and waited. She cleared her throat and spoke softly, just as we do in church or temple or any of our holy places even today.

"Bear People, I have come to you today to make you this offering of honey and to ask a question."

The bears blinked and were silent, waiting. This was their first teaching to Golden Locks, and it was about taking as much time as one requires. The girl did not know if they had heard her or understood her. She did not even know if any of this was truly real, but she continued.

"Bear People, I keep dreaming of you, and so I have come to seek you out. The question I have for you is this, Will you teach me magic?"

The Bear People said nothing and continued their first lesson in teaching her how to wait. And so for a long time, all four figures stood clumped together at the entrance to the cave. For magic takes time and effort and determination. The Bear People were curious. Did the human girl have these traits? Golden Locks waited respectfully. She would not leave and stood with her arms crossed.

Mother Bear was satisfied. So, she shuffled her big frame into the cave, and after a moment, Golden Locks followed. In the center of the cave was the hearth where the bears had their meals. There were three leaves of different sizes piled high with various berries and roots and treasures from the forest.

Here the bears paused, and Mother Bear spoke in a soft and grumbling voice like rocks shuddering in the deep earth. "Why did you come here?"

Golden Locks responded immediately. "My dreams told me to."

Father Bear nodded. "If you want to learn magic, then you must learn to find the right way for you. Which one?" He gestured to the three leaves neatly encircling the hearth.

She went to the first leaf, the largest and the one that was most overflowing with all kinds of delectable Bear People foods. She sniffed it and tasted a berry, considering. She went to the next leaf, softer and full of flowers, roots, and berries. She sniffed it too, inhaling the scent of the flowers so deeply that it went into her bones. Finally, she went to the smallest of the leaves. She picked it up. The roots whispered to her of old knowing and older ways. She spied a raven wing.

Each leaf was lovely. Each unique. But none of them were right for her.

"I shall make my own." And so she did, taking a berry from Father Bear's leaf and a flower from Mother Bear's leaf and an old root from Baby Bear's leaf. She paused, considered, smelled and tasted, thought and felt. Finally, she nodded.

"Now this is just right."

The Bear People said nothing but took her back farther into the cave, where there were three large boulders. Baby Bear hopped up on one of the boulders and sat as nicely as you please.

Mother Bear's husky voice filled the cave once more.

"In magic you have to know when to act and how to wait. Which one?"

The girl sat on the largest boulder, which had an impression in it that reminded her exactly of Father Bear's body. No matter how she shifted, she was barely comfortable. The boulder chair was hard in all places and made her think only of what was difficult and harsh.

She moved to the next boulder, which was decked out in moss and lichen and was a better fit for her size. But as soon as she sat down, she sank into the dry mosses and felt that everything was too soft, gentle, and easy. There was no tension here, and so there could be no balance. Standing up, she brushed the moss from her skirts.

She went to the third boulder. It was covered in deerskin and fox furs and was soft and cozy but still firm. Yet it was also small and carried the scent of Baby Bear, not her own.

So, she moved away a short distance, and using extra leaves and furs and arranging things just so, she made her own place to sit. This new seat had a touch of hardness, like the first boulder and like some of the parts of her life. But the seat also had just a touch of softness, like the second boulder and like other parts of her life. It was warm and safe with its furs, just as she felt now in this cave. She circled around it several times, like a cat, until she was quite sure that it fit her shape precisely. Magic too, she thought, should be like this.

"This one is just right."

Baby Bear was finishing off the honey as the bears took Golden Locks back even farther into their cave. Here the air began to grow warmer, and there was the unmistakable scent of Bear People musk. It was very dark, and Golden Locks began to feel a little fear crawl up her spine, as icy as the river water she had plunged into. Were the Bear People taking her back here to eat her? Had this been the plan all along? Would she be devoured, her quest for magic resulting in a few white bones stripped clean of skin and meat?

Baby Bear nudged her arm and gestured to three dens, which clearly were where each of the Bear People rested at night. His voice was like wind rustling through dry leaves.

"Magic also requires rest and dreaming. Which one?"

Golden Locks went to the first den, which was big and well-appointed and covered in the spicy scent of cedar and evergreen boughs. It smelled delicious here, but the boughs poked at her. This den was too hard, too complicated, and too difficult of a space to manage. So, she moved to the next.

This den was covered in flowers and soft mosses and more lichens like those on the second boulder. They were lovely and soft, but they made her sneeze and itch, and she could not feel the support of the floor. This den was too cloying, too clingy, too undefined.

The third den, like the third boulder, was covered in deerskins and fox furs and was comfortable. She curled up into it but could not fall asleep, for it did not belong to her and did not fit her quite right.

So, she took up some pine boughs from Father Bear's bed, because parts of her story were sharp and clear, and some moss from Mother Bear's bed, because parts of her story were fuzzy and not yet defined, and a fur from Baby Bear's bed, because parts of her story were rich and had come after sacrifice. She circled round and round like a dog, pawing this way and that, until every branch and fold was exactly as she wanted it to be.

"There now. This one is just right."

She snuggled down in her newly created bed, and then she promptly fell asleep. When she awoke a few hours later, a crescent moon shone down its light from a crevice in the roof of the cave, and she was startled to find three pairs of eyes watching her intently. Baby Bear put a honey-sticky paw on her shoulder.

"Now you know magic. Now you know that it is not something you learn but something you remember."

And so, she did.

For a time, Golden Locks stayed with the Bear People, and they talked and sang and danced and told old stories, and she learned much more. Eventually she returned to her village, no longer as Golden Locks, the innocent, sugar-sweet girl-child, but as Headstrong and Heartstrong Woman, with flashing dark eyes.

She did know magic. She knew how to heal, how to help, and how to read signs on the wind and in the woods. And the people loved her, even though she knew that one day they may not, for they were a forgetful people.

But Golden Locks would never forget. She kept those memories safe in story, tied up close to her heart. And she learned the languages of the other peoples of the forest too—the Stone People, the Tree People, the Fox People, the Fish People. And she taught the ones who came after her how to remember their magic. Her teachings were handed down voice to voice, person to person, life to life, with the promise that the ones who make magic would always remember how to talk to bears, and more importantly, they would know how to listen when the bears speak.

And now that is a promise I shall entrust to you. And in return, I shall tell you all about the ways of magic.

REMEMBER YOUR MAGIC

The universe is full of magical things
patiently waiting for our wits to grow sharper.
EDEN PHILLPOTTS, *A Shadow Passes*[1]

Now it is time to remember ourselves, not just a little bit or piece by piece, but wholly and completely. Now it is time to remember our magic. Magic of leaf and root, hearth and home, needle and thread, candle and prayer, feather and fang. Magic that weaves all that is extraordinary back into right relationship to our everyday lives, bridging the ways that we have grown divided—against ourselves and each other. Magic that heals and restores. Much of what you need in order to make this magic you already have in your home. All of what you need to make this magic resides in your brilliant, crimson, beating heart.

Magic is a wild animal. It is hawk and eagle, raven and owl, coyote and fox, wolf and wildcat, badger and bear. It shifts into all of the shapes and forms in between. Magic has been hunted and harried, tortured and trapped. It has witnessed its kin killed and its natural habitats destroyed. And like all wild creatures that find ways against the odds to survive, magic has grown careful and cautious, wise and wily. It is seen only in glimpses—a flash of eye, a swish of tail, a blur of motion—and then we are left with only trees and shadows and stars. It cannot be pursued in the usual ways. It is not something you can buy with money, earn through good behavior, or attain through the heat of drama and risk. The wilderness in which this particular wild animal resides is not found in some faraway and exotic place. It is here, and it is absurdly, wildly, free.

For magic, like the wild itself, is not found in a place we go to. Rather, it resides in the places where we always are. Magic moves through the wilderness of the soul and is found in the soul soil of everyday life and experience. It is found in the doing of the laundry, the making of beds and grocery lists, catching up with friends, having babies, taking lovers, going to school, making money, commuting to work, buying clothes, and cooking dinner. Every single one of these acts has been marked up and down and all around with the paw prints of magic. Each seemingly banal activity bears magic's scent trails and claw marks.

It is hard to see this at first and almost impossible to believe. All mysteries, so we are told, have been discovered, named, bagged, and tagged. There is nothing unknown, nothing of wonder to find here, nothing to see. This conventional wisdom has been the greatest teacher in the present age, and it has taught us incorrectly. A world without wild things is greatly diminished; this we know. The same is true for lives lived without the touch of magic. In all places we look, magic is a mark carrying depth and scope, an essential ingredient for a life well lived.

Magic is present in our earliest civilizations in the form of a dazzling array of rituals, ceremonies, and holy places both made and found. It has moved through all of our great religions, despite what the official teachings and proclamations might say. It has even traveled in surprising places like the roots of rational thought and philosophy fathered by Socrates, a man who heeded a wise oracle and listened to the voice emanating from his soul. When we begin to see all of the places where magic has walked and stalked, denned and fed, we see clearly that it has been with us, loping, running, flying by our side and throughout our daily lives since time beyond time. Where else would we expect to find it if not exactly here in our midst, hiding in plain sight?

For those who would remember their magic and rub up against its electric wildness, a shift in vision and understanding is required, for there have been as many falsehoods spread about magic—what it is and what it is not, where it can be found and where it cannot be found—as there have been about the many wild creatures in the world.

The biggest falsehood is that it is the best, most wonderful, and hope-filled lie ever to be told. Magic makes every fairy tale glimmer and every legend sing, and at the same time, it does not, has not, and cannot exist in the real world, ever—end of story. Yet those who know how to look will discover the prints of magic padding not only throughout our past but also here, tracking through our lives today. Antibiotics, friends you have met through a channel of invisible electrons, the ability to save countless species and to measure harms caused to our lands by our modern advances—all inhabit their own kind of magic.

Some have been taught that magic is found only in arcane teachings that fill dusty grimoires, in constructing a perfect sacred circle, or in the performance of an intricate rite. A parallel thought running alongside these assumptions is that magic is fated to be only an outlaw, an outcast, different, apart, strange, and estranged, as are those who practice it.

One consequence of this thought is that many believe magic is found only in the shocking and bizarre and nowhere else. But in truth, grocery stores, bookstores, local community meetings, and neighborhood parks are just as likely to be natural habitats of magic as grand temples, top-secret ceremonial sites, sacred groves, or underground clubs. This book challenges and calls into question the esoteric occulting, occluding, and mystifying of magic.

Many who seek magic look for it in faraway places and exotic lands, convinced that it has been housed and preserved in its pure form somewhere out there by indigenous peoples and tribes. The hard truth is that no culture exists in pristine form, unfractured, unfragmented.[2] Further corrosion of these already damaged cultures takes place with each attempt to capture, cage, and smuggle out ways, traditions, and practices from their native lands, transplanting them, without thought to harm or health, into unfamiliar habitats that are not made to support them. Appropriation of indigenous cultural practices is often done in the belief that some people in some places have a deeper relationship to the things that matter than we are capable of in our wealthy, developed, formally educated societies. While it is true that there are tribes and communities of people who live within vast wilderness areas with a high diversity of wild creatures, it is also true that access to the wild animal that is magic has never been truly closed—even, sometimes especially, in the most urban concrete-and-asphalt streets or the most urbane boardrooms and classrooms, and even in such unlikely places as the digital realm. Our work is to see this and remember it. Furthermore, we shall come to realize that the intentional or unintentional theft of another person's or people's magic comes at a great cost—the ignorance and neglect of our own deepest good and the harming of those we claim to hold in highest esteem.

Another popular view of magic seeks to domesticate its wildness through the use of psychology, therapy, and self-improvement. Those who view magic solely in terms of literary and psychological insight will find that it is much like having the skin of a wolf and thinking that somehow you have the whole wolf in your hands. Within these pages, we will remember a magic that is wholly fleshed out. This approach speaks to the psychological, therapeutic, and intellectual concerns everyone has, but it will also, as my community members like to say, support us in "getting stuff done," without losing the sense of a magic that is real, wild, and whole. And in this approach, magic does not simply grant us what we wish for or give us what we want—it is a force that drives us to ask why we want what we want and what the best possible choices before us really are.

Finally, there are those who are drawn to magic or who feel the presence of magic shadowing them yet who will not seek out, stay, listen, or learn because they have been taught that magic and spirituality (or magic and religion) are at odds with each other. Underlying this resistance is the idea that in order to make magic we must buy into a certain set of spiritual or religious axioms and beliefs or that the set of axioms and beliefs, the moral codes by which life is lived, are in fundamental opposition to the ways of remembering and making magic. Spirituality and magic are not either-or propositions. They are both-and. Some of the strongest magic I have ever seen has been made by deeply devout souls—Christian, Jew, Buddhist, Hindu, Muslim, and Pagan—each making magic in their own ways.

All of the ways of thinking and learning about magic enumerated above have one thing in common: they assert that magic can be understood only in this one way and no other. Not one of these approaches will tempt magic to share so much as a whisker with us, for magic does not like to be told what to do or where to go. Like all wild creatures, magic shows up anywhere and everywhere. No set of doors, central authority figures, or doctrines can keep it out for long. Magic is the most real part of any "real life," the spark illuminating the authentic core of every experience.

This book is written for *all* people who wish to remember and recover their magic—for the believers and the nonbelievers and those in between, for the formally educated and the informally taught, for those who fall on all sides of the political spectrum, those who have money and prospects and those who lack both. It is written for Witch and Christian, Pagan and Jew, Muslim and Buddhist, Hindu and Atheist alike, for philosophers and artists, moms and dads, businessmen and businesswomen, and rebel-activists. Magic, being the wild creature that it is, does not distinguish in the ways that people do—it is an equal-opportunity adventure.

Before we go off on our trek, it is useful to understand how we came to these misunderstandings of magic and the world. At the beginning of modernity, philosopher and priest René Descartes famously set himself to the earnest demolition of all his beliefs and opinions and began a search for the original foundations of knowledge.[3] And he brought us all along with him. No one alive today is untouched by the far-reaching consequences of his attempt to make a fresh beginning grounded solely in a narrow, highly technical understanding of what reason is. Much of the occlusion of magic we experience today has flowed from these quarters. In order to see the ever-present thread of the extraordinary, we must make a shift out of the Cartesian system undergirding our sense of reality.

This is a shift in the way we see, think, and feel, a shift that entails standing on fresh ground, and it is fundamentally a shift in the way we remember. The stories many of us have inherited about magic must be released and set free: that magic is not real; that magic is fantasy; that magic is exclusive, only found here, only available in these colors and languages, only for men or only for women, only for spiritual attainment or for personal gain.

We must also shift from thinking that it is obvious what magic is or is not. You will notice in this book that I never define magic—not because it has no definite contours but rather to highlight the central importance of seeking the magic that is your own magic. Far from fitting experience into a formula or definition, what we need to do is greet our experiences of magic with wonder, curiosity, and the love we bear for all precious, wild things.

FIELD NOTES, RITUALS, AND STEPPING STONES

Any good seeker must be patient, learning to look and listen with greater care. Over time we begin to gather evidence and clues—a bit of fur here, a track leading off into dense brush over there, and growls and laughs, yips and howls, emerging from deep in the dark of night.

Practically, we will do this work of looking and listening through journaling questions and exercises—taking field notes from both the everyday and the extraordinary. The tools needed will be few: sturdy shoes, a pen in fine working order, a Making Magic journal, which may be any journal or notebook you desire. If it is not difficult to rustle up a friend or two to join you on the quest, then do so, as many of the questions and prompts in this work profit from being shared with true friends. I think of such friends as magical study buddies.

Each chapter contains two rituals to help you deepen your relationship with the vast resources found in the ground of the soul, your soul soil, so that you may better follow the tracks left by the wild creature that is magic. When seeking out wild creatures in natural habitats, we must make an offering of time and attention. When we seek to remember magic, we must make the same offering. The rituals are designed to be moments when you can touch and feel the form of your personal magic in reward for the work, time, and attention that you put into it. These rituals are simple and straightforward and make direct use of the everyday.

The first ritual in each chapter is simpler in terms of process and time, while the second ritual takes a more comprehensive view of the chapter's material and provides various ways to weave it into your own life and experiences.

The ritual guidelines are just that—guidelines. They are not meant to be taken as hard-and-fast rules. In discovering anew your own magic, you may feel called to make changes to each ritual. I actively encourage this kind of creative collaboration, as it is the essence of what it means to make magic.

When engaging in the rituals from each chapter, my recommendation is that you give yourself time and space where you will not be disturbed. But if that isn't for you, fear not. These are rituals that can be performed in many different conditions—including loud and busy ones. Because after all, magic happens *in* life.

Near the end of each chapter there is also a section called "Stepping Stones." Sometimes we do not have the ten-plus minutes that a more formal ritual requires. If you find yourself in that situation, but you want to have some small practice to support yourself in cultivating the ideas from the chapter, then the Stepping Stones section is for you. It offers tiny practices that allow you to take big steps forward. If you are practicing the rituals in each chapter, the Stepping Stones section is a good way to tie the chapter's rituals together to keep your good work going.

Across time and culture, the seeker's journey is traditionally understood to be a spiral path. Why? Because spirals are an apt description of the experience that our souls undergo in their search for truth and beauty: in the experience of a growth in wisdom, in consciousness, we never lose sight of the beginning, our starting point.

Spirals occur in nature and reflect the golden ratio, which speaks with mathematical precision to the possibility of right relationship. Spirals are inscribed in nature's talismans, small and great, from the double helix of our DNA to the greatest mountain. In its very structure, the spiral path combines the straight with the circular. The spiral path, therefore, is the unexpected path, the path that is counterintuitive. At any given moment, it could appear that you are moving backward, in the opposite direction. Seeking the true, seeking our remembered magic, leads to deeper spaces and higher places. Ultimately, in perfect circular motion, the search carries us back to where the journey started. The end is much like the beginning but with the addition of greater depth.

2

MEMORY AND IMAGINATION

[S]he bore nine daughters, all of one mind,
whose hearts are set upon song, and whose spirit is free from care.
HESIOD, "Theogony" (Hugh G. Evelyn-White, translator)[1]

I am often asked how a certain ritual is performed, how an enchantment for this or that might be woven, or how a particular ceremony can be made. In this book, I'm aiming for something more ambitious: to show you the starting points and sources from which all magic is made so that you, as the sacred artist that you are, can learn from your own experience.

How do we begin this process? Well, it is best to go into the wilds with some kind of a guide—the stars, a lamp, a sextant, or a compass. This is no less true when the uncharted wild lands to be explored are the realm of our everyday experiences. So, what or who is the guide that can reveal the starting points of something as timeless as magic?

The answer, the guide, is story. Stories are the primary sources that speak to and for all of the sacred arts, including magic. As we begin to learn how to make magic, we must recover our story and find instructions for the discovery and cultivation of that most essential tool for making magic—not a ritual blade, wand, or candle, but our deepest memory and our most sacred imagination.

Golden Locks lives in a world where human people have forgotten their magic. They've forgotten their magic because they've forgotten their true stories. With the loss of true stories comes the diminishment of both deep memory and the sacred imagination. And with the loss of both comes a loss of connection to the living whole of which we are part. The fragmentation we are so familiar with today has its roots here. The task before Golden Locks and before us, if we choose to accept it, is the same: awaken the deep memory and imagination.

Thus, early in the tale, remembering is indispensable, but it is not quite enough. Golden Locks must indeed remember, but she also must exercise her imagination to accomplish her goal. And she must act. She is successful in large part because she is willing and able to imagine a different ending to the story than the others in her village assume to be the only ending—that the Bear People have nothing to say and will only be interested in how tasty her flesh is. It is here that our exploration must begin as well: with Memory, the mother of the Muses, and her lovely daughters, the Muses of the Imagination, sources of all the deepest and highest inspirations for human beings. The call to remember and imagine the true and good things, whole and sound, to imagine a different ending to our stories, sets us on a course of action to find that wild creature that is our very own magic.

The uncharted terrain through which we travel in this chapter begins with the everyday experience of memory and imagination. You are invited to explore the ways memory and imagination—like the Muses and their mother—are distinct yet, in fact, deeply inseparable powers, not at all divided as we like to think. From this starting point, we will chart a course to what I refer to as the sacred imagination. As I mentioned in chapter 1, in order to catch sight of your very own magic, to sense new possibilities, in order to call the pieces of it back together once more—to literally re-member it—a shift will be required. That shift is made possible by the sacred imagination.

FIELD NOTES FROM THE EVERYDAY

Consider your own experience of the acts and beings involved in memory and imagination—before science enters the picture. Consider what memory and imagination are like from your inner experience—not from the perspective or the studies of cognitive neuroscience or psychology. Science seeks truth and finds it, but the search here is for what supports that truth from within.

Say, for example, that a person weighs 170 pounds, measurable by a standard scale. She may find it difficult or even impossible to pick up 170 pounds of deadweight, if she is not a weightlifter. But how does it actually feel to be 170 pounds? It doesn't feel at all like lifting deadweight. From the inside of her own experience of that 170 pounds, moving about in full health, she feels relatively light—maybe even light as a feather. This is the inner perspective of memory and imagination that we're looking for. Our inner perspective does not cancel out the scientific perspective; they are complementary.

Memory is fascinating. I encourage you to get interested in the ways of your own memory. It has a unity, like our physical bodies or a landscape have a unity, and this unity can be touched or awakened at almost every part or point. In order to remember a particular summer day many years ago, we do not need to go through all of our memories in chronological order or travel in reverse, back through all the years, the way we would need to first turn the corner on North Broad Street to find our way back down the Esplanade to Desoto. Instead, we can call to mind and heart multiple points of contact—including smells, tastes, and sights—that conjure an immediate set of experiences, feelings, and sensations.

Everybody's topography or inner body of memory is unique. To explore yours, start with the surface of things. You don't need to dig down or cut into uncomfortable memories to find what you're looking for here. The topography of our experience with memory from the inside provides plenty of information without strenuous interpretive analysis. Simply start noticing what you normally do not notice: the everyday action of your unique memory. How does memory show up for you and support you every day?

RITUAL   TRACKING MEMORY

This small, simple, but very potent daily mental cultivation ritual has its roots in the practices of ancient Greek philosophers and mystics, as well as in the mindfulness practices of Buddhist lineages. Variations of it are used in therapeutic contexts to support survivors of abuse, war, and trauma of all kinds.[2]

This ritual serves two purposes. First, it heightens your awareness of your relationship to memory and to your experience of the present moments that are distinguishable from and underlie memory. Second, it attunes you to your everyday experiences.

TIME   about 15 minutes

MATERIALS
- ~ your Making Magic journal
- ~ a pen or a pencil
- ~ a timer

PROCESS

Breathe in a blessing on your physical body. Exhale in gratitude.

Set your timer for fifteen minutes and record the events of the previous day, without comment or judgment. Start anywhere—with what happened in the morning, afternoon, or evening. There is no need to try to pick an interesting experience or "problem area" to focus on. Making breakfast, walking down the street, working in the office—all the little, seemingly unremarkable things that happened during the previous day are what you're recording here.

Simply describe what happened or what you were doing in as much detail as possible, including the sights, sounds, and any other details that seem relevant. Don't get into the mental or emotional details of these happenings, such as whether you were worried while you were walking down the street, or whether you were thinking or feeling something profound. Resist the temptation to comment on what happened.

Take your time. When the timer rings, put your writing implement down, even if you are not finished.

Breathe in a blessing on your physical body once more and on your willingness to show up for this work. Exhale in gratitude.

Move forward with your day.

After doing this daily ritual for a week or two, consider what discoveries you have made about your memory. Is it more flexible than you thought, more inexhaustible? If you feel that you have a poor memory, you might discover that, in actual fact, you have a much better memory than you had realized.

BREATH AS BLESSING

All of the *Making Magic* rituals begin and end with the following instruction: "Breathe in a blessing on your physical body." If you have never blessed yourself in this way before, not to worry—it is quite simple.

Breathe in a deep breath, and as you do, bless your physical body in the way that works best for you. You might simply think, "Thank you, blessed body, for being here," or "I love you," or "May you be healed." If it feels right, you may place a hand on your heart, your stomach, or your abdomen to actually feel the breath/blessing as it fills your body.

Exhale completely, acknowledging that releasing your breath fully is as important as breathing in deeply. Upon exhaling, allow yourself to release one thing—big or small—that you can let go of for the rest of the day. After you have exhaled completely, take a moment to feel thanks for your breath and the body it nourishes.

This same blessing breath can be used to bless physical objects, such as special talismans or an altar, and other beings, such as a loved one or an animal friend.

FIELD NOTES FROM THE EXTRAORDINARY

Wild creatures, wild places, and remembered magic all love play. So, as we turn now from memory to imagination, we need to open to the sense of playfulness that is inherent in life. The power of imagination—of our own imagination, as we experience it from the inside—invites us to act the fool. Throughout the many halls of story, fools are often the only ones capable of speaking true wisdom.

Imagination, like memory, responds to personal attention and care. Have a playful conversation with your imagination. What condition is your imagination in? What feeds it? Is it well fed? Does it get plenty of room and space to exercise? Does it have friends?

Here's a hard one: Do you tend to outsource the use of your imagination to TV, books, and movies? Is it filled with words and stories, images and ideas that are not in your best interest? What might your imagination need to shed? Have you spent much time with your imagination over the past year, five years, or thirty? It may be unsettling to realize to what extent we have outsourced our imagination or how neglected or undernourished it is. Don't despair—the waters of imagination run deep, and they can always be set loose to run free and clean once more.

The most primary work in weaving together the ordinary and the extraordinary is the work of deep remembering, or making the shift in perspective that calls us back to the inside of our experience and that involves the play of imagination. Remembering your own magic is not like gazing at a snapshot of the past from the outside; instead, you experience it internally, in such a way that you feel the stirring of its feathers, the ruffling of its fur, and its breath on your neck.

This experience is not mystical exactly. I find that the word *mystical* tends to bring more confusion than clarity, and it conceals what is actually taking place in the ground of your experience, which is simply on the level of feeling your own body weight from the inside.

When we are able to ground ourselves in our individual experiences, we find that remembering and imagining are both at play at the same time. This is what I call the sacred imagination. And it is through the eyes of the sacred imagination, coming back to a sense of life from the inside and remembering, that we are able to prick our ears up and hear the wild calls of magic, find its tracks, and catch its scent.

RITUAL EASY BREATH
RELAX AND RELEASE

This is an exercise I do every morning and also the blessing I begin every teaching with. It speaks to the need alluded to earlier: to release certain things from memory in order to make room to imagine new, correct, and useful experiences and information. You may do this ritual every day, once a day, several times a day, or whenever you have need. Every other ritual I provide in this book begins with this exercise, for I find it to be that fundamental.

TIME   about 10 minutes

PROCESS

Breathe in a blessing on your physical body. Exhale in gratitude.

Take some time to allow yourself to just breathe—a minute or two. Notice if your breath becomes slower or deeper, shallower or faster. Observe without judging, and as you are able, allow your breathing to become slightly deeper and more regular. This is an opportunity for you to learn about the relationship between your body and your breath, the body of your memory and the breath of your imagination, from the inside—that is, the way it actually feels to inhabit breath, body, memory, and imagination.

As you are ready, take in a deep breath, feeling it spiral up from the soles of your feet, through your calves, through your knees, thighs, hips; moving up through your sex, your abdomen, and back; spiraling up from fingertips into palms, into forearms, into shoulders; spiraling up into your chest, your neck, until the breath reaches all the way to the top of your head.

Reflect on how it feels in your body to be so full of nourishing breath. Reflect on how it feels to remember and to allow yourself to daydream, to extend your imagination beyond the limits of the possible.

As you are ready, release that breath. Release it fully and completely, and as you do so, release one thing that you can let go of for the rest of the hour, the day, the week, the month, or the rest of your life. This can be a big thing or a small thing: a concern that the taxes were not done on time, an old story about love, the hurtful thing a child said yesterday, the fact that you haven't talked to your best friend in a week. Whatever it is, just release it for now.

For the purpose of this practice, releasing doesn't mean denying something ever existed or forgetting all about it. Releasing means honoring the distinction and the distance between yourself and whatever it is you have identified as needing to be released. You are remembering that there really is distance, there is space, between you and that. It is not you. You are not it. Discernment is key.

On your next inbreath, breathe in a blessing on yourself. You get to decide what kind of blessing—a blessing of peace, power, strength, brilliance, endurance, joy, prosperity, generosity. You know what you need. Feel into it and say it.

Release your breath, and then breathe in one more blessing on your physical body. Exhale in gratitude.

Move forward with your day.

STEPPING STONES

- Have a conversation with your imagination. Ask it what it needs right now and find out what it has had too much of lately.

- Allow yourself to play—a game, a sport, a character, or a song—just for the sheer joy of it. Take measure of how you feel before letting yourself play and how you feel after.

- Think about the figure of the fool. Many different fools are found in story and drama throughout the world. Which ones are your favorites? Why do you love them?

I will not tell you how to make magic, how to create ritual, how to make ceremony, because it cannot be done. At best, this book can serve as a reminder of what you already know as soon as you begin to look and learn from your own everyday and absolutely extraordinary experiences.

There is no such thing as pure magic; there is only *your* magic. Your task, ever and always, when it comes to making magic is to get it *just right* for you. The wilds of your own life are waiting, and when you discover magic ducking around the corner, it, in turn, has found you. For your very own magic is not only yours—you belong just as surely to it. In wonder and love, embrace it fully and completely with both the everyday and extraordinary acts of life.

3

FINDING THE DOORS

If the doors of perception were cleansed,
every thing would appear to man as it is, infinite.
For man has closed himself up,
till he sees all things thro' narrow chinks of his cavern.
WILLIAM BLAKE, *The Marriage of Heaven and Hell*[1]

The common saying is that any journey begins with just one step. But in fact, all journeys begin with something before the first bold step out into the world: they begin with the daring to find and open the right door.

It is exactly this way for our intrepid storybook heroine Golden Locks. The forest and village are two different realms serving two different purposes, cultivating two different mindsets. The villagers, however, do not ordinarily see this; for them, there is only one realm, their realm of the village. The forest is a stock figure for them, and as such, there is nothing really extraordinary about the forest. It is there all of the time, ever present, surrounding the village, easy to take for granted. Entering and leaving the forest for some might be a daily part of life. But they go into the forest to get what they need, and then they come out to go back home, forgetting all about the forest itself.

Everyone recognizes that the forest marks a boundary of some sort. The question is, What sort of boundary? The animals, the villagers are sure, are out to get human beings. Something dark and dangerous must be lurking there in the shadows. They've made rules about who can and cannot cross that boundary—for example, children, especially little girls, are forbidden from entering. Despite the fact that everyone believes they know what the forest is about, no one *really* knows what happens on the other side of the boundary of the forest. The boundary they know keeps out, keeps at bay, separates the known and familiar from the fearful terra incognita.

Golden Locks sees the forest as a boundary too, but the sort that is a door, a boundary of connection and meaning, an opening and marker that both distinguishes and relates. Determined to remember and seek out magic, she does the only sound thing there is to do: she opens the door and steps through it.

Doors, when they are found, work in precisely the same way that the forest in the story does for Golden Locks and for all who see such forests truly. And, like the forest, these doors are all around us, hiding in plain sight, as magic tends to do. In this chapter, you are invited to explore the doors hidden in plain sight in your own experience—the doors that open to the extraordinary.

FIELD NOTES FROM THE EVERYDAY

Think for a moment of all the doors you pass through every day. Most of the time we hardly notice these doors. So few of them are, after all, made to be noticed. They are made so that it is easy to pass through them, as quickly as possible, in order to get to the other space, the other side, no matter where it is, with minimal obstruction and fuss.

The doors are as many as are the destinations we travel to and from. Our front doors take us out of the comfort and safety of our homes and out into the wide world, where we are faced with the general public and the demands and obligations of daily life. The car or bus or subway doors take us into the frenetic activity of movement and transportation, where we have to be focused, paying attention, aware of the traffic around us. When we walk through the doors of our offices and jobs, we often feel ourselves standing up straighter, invisibly surrounding ourselves with the layers of armor required for our various workplaces, so that we are able to give off the vibes of competence, creativity, good cheer, or professionalism. When we exit that door at the end of our workday, we carry with us an often quite different set of feelings, sensations, and thoughts. We might be happy with the way the day went or worried about a project; maybe we feel drained and unsatisfied. But whatever our experience is, we know that we are different coming out of the workplace at the end of the day than when we went into it. Even those of us who work from home and have a ten-second commute from the bedroom to our desks experience this transformation.

Reflect on these most normal and usual activities of opening doors, closing doors, moving through them and over their thresholds. Become a connoisseur of the experience, tasting it, as it were, with every part of the tongue. Remember the example of body weight in chapter 2 and the difference between deadweight and what that same weight actually feels like from the inside. What happens when you are moving from one space into another? What is it like? What changes do you undergo physically, emotionally, and mentally? Are there doors in life right now that you love to go into or out of, or even to pass by, just to see them? Are there doors that you already associate with deeper meaning, with magic? Likewise, are there doors that create anxiety or worry for you? These are the physical outer doors that you have daily experience with. What do they teach you?

Everything begins with simply noticing. If you start to notice what it is like to pass through different doors and into and out of the different spaces they separate, you will notice that every time you enter and exit through a door, something within you shifts and changes. It is a subtle but present shift. You may be noticing it for the first time.

Reflection is itself a door. New sensations, new meanings, new possibilities open up with this caring attention to the everyday experience of doors and the spaces they connect. How is it possible that as you exit certain doors you feel so tired? Who knew that going through the door of our favorite grocery store could bring so much sensual pleasure? Be prepared for discovery as you reflect on the magic of doors in your life.

RITUAL ATTENDING TO YOUR THRESHOLD

This small ritual gives some basic suggestions for attending to the threshold that you most frequently cross on the way into and out of your home. The suggestions here are optional and really meant to trigger your imagination into finding what techniques and little magics are just right for you and your door.

TIME   10 to 30 minutes

MATERIALS
- ~ your Making Magic journal
- ~ a small table
- ~ a bottle of your favorite perfume or room spray
- ~ flowers or other special objects (optional)
- ~ a basket for shoes (optional)

PROCESS

Perform the "Easy Breath Relax and Release" found in chapter 2.

Consider the door to your home that you enter and exit through the most. This could be the back door, front door, or door leading from your garage to your house.

Stand outside of it.

Go inside.

Go back outside.

Take a few moments to reflect in your Making Magic journal on how you feel opening, closing, and going through this door.

Now, set up a small table just inside your home by the entrance to your door. Place a bouquet of fresh flowers or a living plant on it. Add any other items that you would love to see and experience when you first come in—maybe a small piece of artwork or a pretty rock you found on a walk. Add a bottle of your favorite perfume or room spray. Set the basket for shoes, if you are using one, underneath the table or to the side of it.

Once you have set things up *just right*, go outside once more. When you enter your home, use the perfume or room spray to spray the air around you lightly. As you pass through the scent, deeply breathe in the blessing "I am home." Take your shoes off and place them in the basket.

You will experience small but noticeable differences after making these changes. How does it feel to do these things as you enter your home? Keep track of what you notice. Don't analyze; simply note in your Making Magic journal what those differences feel like. What do they tell you about this particular door and your relationship to it?

FIELD NOTES FROM THE EXTRAORDINARY

The phenomenon we are approaching through the everyday experience of doors is what we can call *liminal*. The word *liminal* derives from the Latin *limen*, which means "threshold." Our everyday experience of doors and thresholds teaches us about the nature of the liminal, the way worlds are deeply woven together here, now, and always.

Now the task is to find the doors that point to the liminal in your everyday experience. Look sharply and listen well, for these doors can be anything—the wooden gate outside the house leading to the street, the glass door you pass through as you hurry into the restaurant on your first date, the elevator door that snicks shut and takes you down to the lobby where you bump into that old friend you had just been thinking about. But often, like the wild animal that is magic, these doors are hiding, camouflaged, invisible. You may find a door in the necklace your mother gave you, in the color red, in the tree in your front yard, in a twine of thorny roses on black metal, in the sun on your skin.

Think about some of your favorite physical objects right now. Perhaps you have a list of them a mile long, or perhaps only one or two come to mind. Do you know why you love them? What do they mean to you? What do they open you up to? Where do they take you? How do you change, even in the slightest way, in their presence? What about them feels good and makes you happy? If an object comes to mind, don't disregard it because it is not noble or sophisticated enough. Crayons, a plastic spider ring that your seven-year-old gifted you, a beer bottle, an old gaudy ashtray, or a guitar pick are just as likely to be doors leading into the extraordinary as a hand-carved magic wand or a golden key.

Liminal doors can be physical objects, but they may also be places and spaces. What places are deeply resonant for you? What feels special about them? What happens to you when you are there? If there are specific places that are doors for you, take some time to learn about them. Who lived there originally? What languages were spoken there? What are the plants and animals that call this place home now? How was the place cared for, tended, and honored in times past? What ceremonies and sacred stories have been told about it?

Your liminal doors are made of light and shadow, breath, physical movement of all kinds, touch and sensation. Play itself can be a door, as can the erotic. Food and drink, feast and merriment, can be doors. The scents of oils, perfumes, candles, wet grass, electricity that is in the air before a big storm—all can be powerful doors. The sounds that speak to you, that soothe and bless you, the sounds that inspire and energize you—all have the capacity to be doors. Music, spoken-word poetry, books and stories read out loud—all doors. Wind rustling through trees, insects buzzing in the grasses, owls singing in deepest night—all doors.

Sensual doors are often best explored by considering the sensations they inspire. What pleases you and brings you pleasure? What does that pleasure teach you about yourself? Where do you find deep nourishment? Where do you encounter beauty that steals your breath away? What sensual experiences bring about an abiding sense of peace and calmness? What sensual encounters feel overtly magical and mystical? Asking and following these questions faithfully will lead you to discover the particular liminal doors that constellate in the spaces of the everyday.

The doors are everywhere, but, like the faeries in stories, they are very good at hiding. The only way to find them is to get a feel for them. We simply have to know them for what they are and be prepared to find out which ones we need to enter and which shall remain closed for us. Just as we find and open doors to our homes and offices, our schools and studios, we find and open the doors that lead us into the extraordinary.

RITUAL DRESSING AND BLESSING YOUR DOOR

This ritual may be performed at any door or window. It is both protective and a blessing in nature, and it is meant to honor the passages that you physically move in and out of the most. Begin with the door(s) that you use the most and then apply the same process to other doors or windows.

Dressing is a term we find in various folk magic traditions, and it means to magically fix up an object, like a candle, crystal, or door. Typically, the act of dressing an object involves the use of any or all of the following: oil, incense or sacred smoke, prayer and blessing, natural materials like botanicals and minerals.

TIME   20 to 30 minutes

MATERIALS
   ~ your Making Magic journal
   ~ salt
   ~ olive oil, almond oil, or the
     anointing oil of your choice

PROCESS

Perform the "Easy Breath Relax and Release" found in chapter 2.

Stand in front of the door that you come in and out of the most—a door you want to bless and protect. Look at it from the inside and the outside. Notice the details. Does it need a fresh coat of paint? An entry rug or a doormat? Does the area around the door need to be cleaned or spruced up in any way? (See the "Attending to Your Threshold" ritual earlier in this chapter for more inspiration.) What would make your experience of entering and exiting through this door more pleasurable and meaningful?

Take a few moments to make any notes in your Making Magic journal. If there are specific things that you need to do, such as giving the door a new coat of paint or putting some nice plants on either side of it, then go ahead and do them or make a plan to do those things.

When you are ready, sprinkle a bit of salt along the inner and outer thresholds of the door. You do not need to use much—just a pinch. Salt possesses the virtue of purifying, cleansing, and preserving the space around the door so that you are less likely to bring in attitudes, behaviors, ideas, thoughts, and feelings that are not needed or wanted in your space. You may also create a saltwater solution that can be sprayed or sprinkled along the threshold of the door. (For more about the powers of salt, see chapters 8 and 11.)

Take a moment to breathe into the space and acknowledge the door that you pass through so often. When ready, take the oil and pour it into the palm of your hand, allowing it to gently warm. Anoint the four corners and center of your door on both sides with the intention that all who enter and exit through the door are blessed and protected. You may say words straight from your heart during this ritual, or you may say the following blessing: "May all who enter come in love and depart in peace."

What effect does performing a ritual like this have on you? Find out for yourself. You might try doing the ritual several times throughout a given period of time—say, one week. Starting at the beginning of a week of performing the ritual, notice and keep track of how you feel. How have your feelings changed by the end of the week? How does passing through your newly blessed door make you feel? How does simply having a blessed entrance and egress make you feel about your dwelling space and its surrounding environs?

After you've given yourself a period of time actively doing the ritual, follow it up with the same period of time doing nothing. Use these contrasting periods of ritual activity and inactivity as an opportunity to reflect on your experience from the inside. Which period feels better to you and why? Do you find that periods of ritual activity and inactivity support each other, like an inbreath and an outbreath?

STEPPING STONES

- Using photos from magazines or an app like Pinterest, make a physical or a virtual collage of doors, portals, and entryways that you love. Notice what themes, colors, objects, and forms you gravitate to.

- Have you had any meaningful experiences with a door, portal, or entryway? What were they? Jot down the notes in your Making Magic journal. And remember that the doors don't have to be from "real life." One of the doors that made a huge impression on me as a child was the wardrobe that led to Narnia in C. S. Lewis's novel *The Lion, the Witch, and the Wardrobe.*

• Practice opening and closing your front door. How do you feel when it is open? Do parts of yourself open up when you open it? How do you feel when it is closed?

Making magic calls out what is already there, what is dormant and in a state of potency. Magic is the wild creature that is hidden in plain sight—the luna moth dwelling among green leaves, the white wolf curled in the snow. Magic knows how to make good use of camouflage, and it takes on the appearance of many an everyday object and experience.

Our doors are everywhere and part of the everyday. Every moment and each situation presents to us golden opportunities to find our doors and do the only thing that really makes sense: step through them, into the extraordinary. Little and big, subtle and powerful, every door tells a story and every door shows a path—to the possibilities, choices, and wisdom that can arise only from being rooted in both worlds. This includes the everyday doors, the ones we started with, the doors to our own home, and it encompasses all of the other, in many cases unlikely, liminal doors that we discover along the way.

The door is now open between the worlds of everyday and extraordinary, so let us explore a specific place those two worlds meet: in our treasures, our touchstones, our talismans.

4

TREASURES AND
TOUCHSTONES

It is never apart from you right where you are.

DŌGEN, "Fukanzazengi" (Norman Waddell and Masao Abe, translators)[1]

Go out into any wilderness—the woods near your home, the asphalt-covered basketball courts down the street, the middle of the desert where there seems to be nothing for miles and miles, or the city park down the road—and you will find them. If you are paying attention, it is nigh impossible to return home without having found a treasure, a touchstone. It might be a leaf, a piece of glass formed into a sphere by the passing heat of a train, an iron nail, or a single feather.

You may decide to carry your treasure back home with you, or you may leave it in place, simply recognizing it for what it is. With every little object that sings with significance, we are tracking the wild animal that is our magic. We are gathering evidence of it, spotting the trail of breadcrumbs that leads us home to ourselves once more.

For Golden Locks, her treasure is her headband. Made and blessed by her mother, this object is so potent it is the inspiration for her name. It is physical evidence and an indication of how she is seen and known in the wider world. Her headband speaks not only to her name as Golden Locks, but the kind of talisman it is—a headband in particular, something encircling her head—also speaks to her deeper quest: to know, to understand, to learn magic, and most fundamentally, to remember *her* magic. These are all activities of the mind, as well as the heart. By the end of the story, the talisman and Golden Locks herself have undergone a transformation: she becomes Headstrong and Heartstrong Woman. But she begins as Golden Locks, and her own treasure and touchstone, her headband, sketches out through its full circle the path she follows back to herself and her remembered magic.

When we are in actual uncharted territories—be they urban cityscapes, open prairies, or suburban mazes—we both look for and create our own signposts and landmarks to help us get our bearings and orient ourselves to the next steps in our journey so that we may reach our intended destination. In this chapter, we are going to consider the seemingly ordinary objects that we find, inherit, make, or are gifted with and that we carry throughout our lives. We will move from our everyday understanding of them as treasures and touchstones into the deeper realization that they are actually some of the oldest sacred arts tools—magical talismans. We will recover the deep knowing about how to work with, develop, and find our magical talismans, and in the process, we will find yet another way in which the everyday and the extraordinary come together.

FIELD NOTES FROM THE EVERYDAY

For where your treasure is, there your heart will be also.[2] We all have objects that hold special meaning for us—our own personal touchstones, our findings. What are yours? Lucky pennies, two-dollar bills, handwritten notes, a tube of your favorite lipstick, cuff links, special dice, a piece of driftwood, or a stone smoothed by the river. In many cases, we carry these objects with us in our pockets. We tuck them into our wallets and purses. We wear them or place them on our desks, our mantles, or our bedside tables. We hang them from our rearview mirrors. We find them in visual art, hear them in song, and sense them in story.

Not only objects but also symbols or designs can constitute a little finding. Colors, scents, and flavors all possess this ability. All memorable brands and logos are built around this fact: color, form, shape, and feel have the ability to speak on multiple levels at the same time. When we view these objects, symbols, and designs—all of our treasures—through the eyes of remembered magic, our personal relationship with them begins to change. No longer are they simply touchstones kept out of affection, sentiment, or superstition. Instead, these little findings are imbued with a meaning and a purpose. The breadcrumbs we've gathered turn out to be talismans, pointing us to purpose.

Pick a favorite object. It can be anything, as long as it is a favorite little something of yours. Maybe you already view it as a talisman or maybe you don't; it does not matter at this point in time.

Begin by describing the object. Grab your Making Magic journal and use your words. What does the object look and feel like? Does it have a scent? A taste? What do you associate with it? What is the story behind this object or symbol? Why is it meaningful to you? Why have you kept it around? Do you do anything particular with it? Do you use it in any special way or during any special time? Is it a reminder for you? If so, what does it remind you of? Does it point to a specific goal or desire that you have for yourself? If so, what? Consider that goal or desire in turn. What does it point to? Why is it important for you to achieve or master or attain? What is the meaning behind it? What is the real purpose of that goal or desire?

Write down your field notes to these prompts and discuss them with your magical study buddy if you have one.

Next, you may want to take an inventory of all of the special objects you have around you. Start anywhere. Desks are often loaded with these treasures and touchstones, as are bedside tables, mantles, and bookshelves. Perhaps your special object is a favorite lamp or a special piece of furniture. Just make a quick list in your journal of some of the significant objects around you. After you have done so, do you notice any patterns, connections, or striking similarities or differences between the objects?

Far from breaking all attachments to material things, our investigation leads into the heart of those attachments. Let us find out what makes them really special and, in so doing, see where they lead us.

As you survey your various treasures and touchstones, you may begin to discover that each object is significant in a slightly different way, that each one calls to mind different memories and stirs your imagination in a unique manner. You may also discover that some of your treasures and touchstones feel like doors that open up to the liminal, like signposts that encourage you to peer into this part of the trees or under that part of the brush as you seek out your magic. Or they are reminders of what you hold most dear, give first priority to, and tend to focus on. In all of these ways, our everyday treasures and touchstones become something more: they become *magical talismans*.

When treasures and touchstones become pointers to deep purpose, a talisman is born. For all of the different forms talismans may take, each one speaks to our own most cherished goals and aims. The root of the word *talisman* comes from the ancient Greek word *telos*, meaning "end, purpose, for the sake of which." In the everyday structure of things, everything has an aim—all human arts and activities, all beings in the world we inhabit. We find this idea across the world in various traditions. It is not a doctrine but simply a description of our everyday, common experience.

Each of us has purpose too. What drives us throughout our lives and forms our aspirations is so personal, so intimate to each of us, that not only can no one tell you what your purpose is, but also no one can take it away from you. Your sense of deep purpose may be the dearest possession you have—the greatest power, the source of the greatest strength. Sooner or later, you will notice when you've strayed away from it. It may take years for you to notice, but very likely, all around you there will have been signs, marks along the trail telling you that you have become separated from that purpose. One such mark is the yearning that you cannot identify or put into words—the heavenly hurt.

Fortunately, the keys to bringing our lives back into accordance with our purpose are also all around us. And among those keys are those little treasures and touchstones, those talismans, that we have kept nearby all this time.

Talismans are intimate cynosures writ small, pointing the way to the highest or fullest reason for our existence. With talismans, we never start big but always small, one droplet at a time. As Japanese Zen master Dōgen once put it, in a different context, they are like dewdrops of water, reflecting the luminous moon.[3]

RITUAL TALKING TO YOUR TALISMANS

This little ritual provides simple guidance for how to talk to a talisman. You perform it over a seven-day period, so you can go as slowly and gradually as you want.

Did I say *talking*? I sure did! In this ritual, you will allow yourself to put into play your sacred imagination; you will allow yourself to engage in a form of sacred play.

If you feel resistance to this ritual, then when you perform the "Easy Breath Relax and Release," I recommend you release that resistance and let yourself explore.

TIME 10 to 20 minutes

MATERIALS

~ your Making Magic journal
~ the talisman you previously described in your
   Making Magic journal (see page 49)

PROCESS

Perform the "Easy Breath Relax and Release" found in chapter 2.

Consider the talisman you have chosen to work with. Hold it if it can be held. Look at it if it is meant to be looked at. If it has a scent, smell it. If it is something you wear, then wear it.

Affirm and acknowledge that you really wish to get to know it, learn from it, and understand what it has to show and tell you about yourself—the practical, the magical, and all that is in between.

Over the next seven days find a way to be in relationship with your talisman every day.

By addressing your talisman with this sense of play, you are reframing your relationship to this "inanimate" object—what you likely consider a "dead" thing. With the sense of play that only you can embody, let your talisman become a friend, an ally, a companion. As it does, what does it tell you? What does it really want you to know and understand—about yourself, your magic, your experience of both the everyday and the extraordinary?

Feel free to ask your talisman questions. Remember, no one else is listening; magic shows up when you do. How does your talisman want to be taken care of? What are the best ways for you to work with it? Perhaps your talisman even has a specific name it wants you to call it. What might that name be?

Note down your reflections in your Making Magic journal. If you feel like you need more structure to this ritual, you can actually write down specific questions for your talisman in your journal before you spend time with it. Then when you are with it and paying attention, you may note the responses that come to you.

FIELD NOTES FROM THE EXTRAORDINARY

The disconnection between thought and desire and action that occurs in our everyday experience is related to the apparent divide between the everyday and the extraordinary. This is a fact that cannot be overstated. The quite common experience of wanting one thing and doing something completely opposite is that fracture written in miniature that we experience every day. It causes breakage and rifts between peoples and places, and it sounds, from the tiniest cry to the loudest keening, throughout Creation. It is this rift that calls us so urgently to remember our magic here and now, to begin making magic, for it is only through this kind of deep remembering and recollecting of self that we discover ways of mending and repairing.

The Oracle at Delphi spoke to this dissonance eloquently through the inscription above her cave, which read, "Know thyself" and "None too much."[4] The first part of her sage advice recommends not only that we know what we want, what our goals are, what we are aiming toward in our everyday lives but also that the deeper meaning and purpose that underlie those practical desires, goals, and aims become plain as day to us. Why do we want what we want? Find out the answer.

The second part of the imperative, "none too much," reminds us not to get lost in never-ending navel-gazing or second- and third-guessing about our real motivations. Know what you want, and know why you want it. Come to know it in the way you know your best friend. Seasoned magical practitioners often refer to this as creating an intention, but having an intimate knowledge of what we want and why goes far beyond intending something. It is more than a yearning. It is a sense of purpose and of proportion. It is an organizing principle, or *telos*. And our talismans speak directly to it.

In many old magical traditions, there is an understanding expressed thusly: the curse contains the cure. This ancient idea also shows up in literature and in the fact that in one of the old mother tongues, ancient Greek, the word for "poison," *pharmakon*, also means "medicine." At the root of our sense of purpose are both a wound, a broken place, and the possibility of complete healing, of blessing.

The broken places are different for each of us. No two stories are alike, and each is as unique as the individual who bears its scars, which spread out in dendritic patterns and show up on the surface of life in the forms of feeling thwarted and stymied and frustrated. Yet the stories are all striking in their similarities as well—telling how difficult broken places are to detect, often hiding right beneath the surface, and carrying the sense that from this hurt, this wound, there can be no recovery.

Magic tells a different story: every curse holds its cure; every broken place carries within it a deep blessing, a hope. The deeper the wound, the bigger the benediction, and no broken place is too great, too terrible, to keep brave blessings away.

Talismans make this story evident. They are called upon in magic because of their ability to take the richness of practical need and want, the depth of meaning and sense of purpose, and the undeniable presence of our broken places and the blessings that are found within them, and to distill that wealth of story, experience, feeling, and thought into a specific form—a symbol, a shape, a color, a tangible object. That is why no matter what their spiritual and religious affiliations, no matter their belief systems, no matter their superstitions or lack thereof, every person possesses treasures and touchstones. We begin collecting them as children, and as we surround ourselves with them throughout adulthood, we learn from them always.

RITUAL TALISMAN CONSECRATION RITUAL

The word *consecrate* means "to make something sacred." (And *sacred* here should be understood in the way that *you* understand it. What matters most and means the most to you?) To consecrate anything—a talisman or a specific tool or a newborn child—is to confer blessing and protection upon it and to bear witness to its deep meaning and purpose, its *telos*. In this case, our consecration method makes use of the physical body and the four classical elements of earth, air, fire, and water, which are found both within and without.

TIME   about 15 minutes

MATERIALS
- ~ your Making Magic journal
- ~ fragrant smoke (You may use an incense that you like; dried cedar, juniper, bay leaf, or frankincense are all good choices for this ritual.)
- ~ a small taper candle (optional)
- ~ the talisman you previously described in your Making Magic journal (page 49)

PROCESS

Perform the "Easy Breath Relax and Release" from chapter 2. If you wish to work with a candle, you may light it now.

Take a few moments to consider how you would like to bless and protect this talisman. You may want to speak this blessing aloud or write it down in your Making Magic journal.

When you are ready, place your talisman in your hand or against your heart. You may say out loud or inwardly, "By the earth of my body, may this talisman ever connect me to discernment in my practical actions."

Breathe in a blessing on yourself and your talisman, and exhale in gratitude.

Next, breathe across the talisman. You may say out loud or inwardly, "By the air of my breath, may this talisman ever connect me to wisdom and the ability to see my desires clearly."

Breathe in a blessing on yourself and your talisman, and exhale in gratitude.

Anoint your talisman with a tiny bit of your saliva. You may say out loud or inwardly, "By the water of my body, may this talisman ever connect me to compassion for myself and others."

Breathe in a blessing on yourself and your talisman, and exhale in gratitude.

Finally, light whatever incense or sacred smoke you are using for this ritual and pass it over your talisman. You may say out loud or inwardly, "By the fire of my spirit, may this talisman ever be a beacon shining bright for me."

Breathe in a blessing on yourself and your talisman, and exhale in gratitude.

Conclude the ritual by sitting with your talisman and considering the deep purpose it brings to your magic-making.

STEPPING STONES

- Identify a special treasure or touchstone and consider what role it has played in your life. Pay special attention to how you feel when you call upon it and what adventures it has accompanied you on.

- Go on a talisman-hunting journey. Think about a specific situation that you would like to have a touchstone for and then go out on a mission to find the just-right object.

- For one week, carry on your person an object that you are especially drawn to. At the end of the week, consider how your week went and what the object's presence added to your experience.

Magic demands that we ask about our own sense of deep purpose, our true north, remembering that to make such an inquiry is to confront both broken places and the blessing ways that pour forth from them.

Among their other qualities, talismans are forces of definition. They define a specific place where the everyday and the extraordinary are woven together and, in turn, allow us to participate in that weaving. Sometimes they define specific doors that mark the threshold of the extraordinary. Always they support us in defining where we are in any given moment, making clear our needs, wants, desires, and also making clear the deeper sense of purpose and *telos* that animates our lives and the daily choices that we make. When it comes to exploring the terrain of our soul, this definition is deeply appreciated and necessary, which is why we often carry our talismans on our physical bodies—as literal touchstones. This definition of where we are is also necessary because so many other aspects of the wilds in which we find ourselves—such as time—refuse to be made tangible or easily defined.

5

TAKING YOUR TIME

When we work at the threshold between the everyday and the extraordinary and engage in both worlds, we make a discovery about time: it too is touched by wild magic. Golden Locks reminds us of this. She has a powerful dream that tells her to go and seek out the ways of magic, to seek out and talk to the Bear People. Does she sit around, plaiting her hair and waiting until Jupiter is just so or the season of autumn has officially started? No! She sets out that day, that morning, listening to her magical instincts, which inform her that *now, now, now* is the time to seek out what needs to be sought. The story calls on us to remember this most critical aspect of the relationship between magic and time: *any* time can be the best time, the *just-right* time, if we know how to look and how to work it.

Everyday doors, treasures, and touchstones have the ability to open out and into the vastness of things that have been held in word and song, carved in stone, drawn in pigment, danced, and dreamt—"time out of mind," as C. S. Lewis calls it.[2] We begin to see how, in order for our weaving of the everyday and extraordinary to take place most potently, we need to be firmly planted in both worlds. Liminal work, in order for it to be truly liminal, must preserve the threshold. It does not lose itself in the "other side," because the other side is only discovered in relationship with our everyday experience. Thus, if you would seek out magic, you must commit to holding that space betwixt and between.

The betwixt and between spills over from space into time, for the act of holding the liminal space puts you in a relationship with a liminal time that embraces the past, present, and future. But to truly preserve the threshold, we must not lose our most everyday ordinary experience of time. So it is that we turn to the territory of time and our lived experience of it. One of the most basic experiences we have—besides the creeping sense that there is never enough time—is procrastinating, putting off what could be done today, here and now, for tomorrow. We might be tempted to think that because the work of seeking and making magic is deep, great, subjective, or interior, we need to wait until there is enough time and space to begin the journey. We might think we need two weeks, six weeks, a full month of vacation time, before we can really go off and start seeking our highest purpose in the wild lands. Soul-seeking and magic-making are not things we can do, we tell ourselves, during regular business hours. But actually they are, if only we know how to start small and follow the times. In fact, that is the only time to begin—with the time and the times that we live in, the time that is deeply familiar for each of us.

FIELD NOTES FROM THE EVERYDAY

Our everyday experience of different worlds (such as home, work, grocery store, highways, and parks) is a dynamic jewel placed in the ever-moving setting of time. But because time is so ubiquitous a presence, it is easy to take it for granted.

For most of us, our days are run on relatively tight schedules. We get up and go to sleep at the same time or thereabouts. We show up to work at a consistent time, and hours later we leave. We drop off and pick up children at specific times. Even meals, times of togetherness, and times of leisure are more tightly scheduled than ever. Time-telling devices are adjusted to a global standard and have grown in power and presence over the years as well. Most technological devices can function as clocks, alarms, timers, stopwatches, and appointment notification centers all at the same moment. Everywhere there are reminders of each passing minute. Not only have we become more aware of time, we have collectively become more rigid about it as well.

Most of us assume that we know what time is, and so we rarely think of time as possessing magical potential. As we grow older, time so often feels like a growing burden, an increasing deadweight that crushes what is most precious in us. We yearn to be released from this soul-crushing weight. But when we experience the *inside* of time—when we experience time in terms of what it is really like to be in it—something interesting happens. The deadweight of time that we have been carrying, this narrowly confined space we yearn to escape from, becomes as light and as buoyant as a rubber ball floating on water, as spacious as the great sky into which a flock of birds takes flight. We discover that it has been light and buoyant all along.

What we have become so painfully aware of in the twenty-first century is only a certain kind of time—a kind of reflection or shadow or tiny part of time—instead of the whole of it, the genuine article. But with just a slight shift in our perspective, the innumerable time-telling devices can be yet another set of doors.

Beginning to see time correctly will lead you to take back or recover your own true time, because you will discover that there is, after all, more than enough time for you to do what you need to do in this life. Time seems to be the scarcest of resources, but it turns out to be among the most superabundant of resources. We are living in a state of poverty amid riches.

The starting point, as always, is your own experience and reflections. Look directly into what you actually find in your own affairs. Be faithful to your discoveries, following them to the end, wherever they may lead. Imagine what your experience of life would be like with this one small change, another way of feeling about the same thing, time—feeling it from the inside. What if you regularly lived in the sense that you have enough time to do what really needs to be done in your heart of hearts? What would change? What would stay the same?

Consider your relationship to time and to the ways that you would naturally mark time. It might be helpful to keep track of your reflections by writing them down periodically in your Making Magic journal.

What timepieces or chronometers do you have in your life? Do you have one or two main devices you use to tell the time? Do you rise with the sun? If not, how and when do you awake, and what do you do upon first waking? What thoughts or feelings do you typically wake up with? Do you go to bed when the moon is at its zenith? If not, how and when do you go to bed, and what do you do before you go to bed? Do the hours of needed sleep and wakefulness and rest change for you during different times of the year? What about one of our most intimate relationships with time—our age? The number we attribute to our age marks the passage of time. What is your actual relationship to your age? What does that number mean to you?

These questions about your actual relationship to time will themselves require some time and awareness, but perhaps not as much as you think. Do not be satisfied with a vague sense of what you routinely do upon waking or falling asleep, but try to become aware of specific changes. The aim, again, is to make that small shift in perspective, from the outside experience of time to the inside experience of it, and to notice what that inside experience of time is actually like for you.

Go beyond the clocks and watches. Consider the larger patterns that alert you to the passing of time, the seasons. Allow yourself to move out of the fixed idea of four seasons when thinking about these patterns. Give up the notion of what seasons should be like, and discover what they actually are in the places that you live. In South Central Texas, where I live, for example, we do not have a true winter; rather, we have a mild autumn for a solid five months. Other locales have longer winters and springs or autumns and summers. What is the relationship between passing seasons and time as you have come to know it?

Do not be afraid to get specific. I have lived in places where there is mesquite-blooming-last-frost season, cottonwood-cotton-drifting-on-the-air season, tadpole-birthing season, first-mockingbird-song season, and redbud-sugar-making season. I didn't make them up. I've observed them emerging straight from the land itself. They mark the various and usually fairly subtle transitions in weather patterns, temperature, and even the number of daylight hours available during a given time of year.

In addition to the seasons, reflect on the seasonal celebrations that are part of life. Again, get specific and think on your actual relationship to them, not on how you are supposed to feel or on how they are supposed to look. For some people, late December is a time filled with warmth and cheer, but for many others it is something altogether different. What is your experience?

From the ways of marking each day and the seasonal transitions, move to considering what holidays—literally holy days—speak to you. What holidays do you love? What holidays make you cringe? Are there holidays that you wish were more fully celebrated and honored or holidays you would like to see vanish altogether? Consider the holidays that you observed and celebrated as a child. Disregard, for the moment, whether you "believe" in the religious framework that surrounds certain holidays. Just look at the day itself, the way you celebrated it and the way that observing it made you feel. Write down a list of your favorite holidays in your Making Magic journal with some quick notes as to why these particular days resonate for you. If a holiday is a so-called secular holiday, like Halloween, Labor Day, or Earth Day, do not let that keep you from noting it. Write it down with a few notes about why you love it and what it means to you.

Every holiday we celebrate can be traced back through its roots to a holy day of some kind. In many cases, the dates are slightly different from one another, so there is not a one-to-one correspondence. In other cases, several festivals and holy days celebrating similar themes cropped up around the same time, or near enough to each other, that they became conflated. But when we look deeply enough, we do find that our holidays have ancient and sacred roots. Some of us will have reactions to holidays that do not fit with the official expectations. Christmas and Yuletide, for example, are often depicted as wonderful times of celebration and socializing as we celebrate new births, a new sun, and miracles in the desert. And yet for many of us, these holy days mark a deeply liminal period; there is something quiet and still about them that makes them ideal for making magic. For others, they are supremely depressing times of year, when rest and the company of one or two good friends are the best medicine.

As you begin to unpack, reflect, and hold to the actual relationship you have with what underlies time, you can easily see and feel that there is not a single monolithic, absolute time. (Or if there is such a monolithic time, the nature of it is far more flexible and giving than the poverty of our thinking has allowed.) It is not uncommon to find a person who is eighty years old, feeling twenty years old. The reason for this is that they are feeling the *inside* of the experience of time. There is nothing fancy here, but there is something that is felt subjectively. The calendar is a method of measurement and tells us something. But any single method of measurement does not give us the true picture. What is happening in the case of our eighty-year-old is that this person is feeling the greater reality of time; they have a fuller and truer picture of what time *truly* is, in the same way that the feeling of our weight from the inside tells us more about what it is like to be 170 pounds.

Our lives are composed of many times. A community is constituted by numberless times. What would our experience of time start to become if we could recognize this—that there is not one arrow of time but many different times? This is a wilder way of seeing time; it is a view of time touched by magic.

With this shift of perspective, our feelings about time might begin to change in small but noticeable ways. We might begin to find that we have just a little more time in our days. This is the consequence of beginning to build our personal knowledge that what is actually needed is not more time but a deeper awareness of the actual times we inhabit. This awareness, in turn, speaks to a fuller sense of spaciousness throughout the days and nights. With such an awareness of time, we may cease being worried that we are late, late, for a very important date, like the White Rabbit in *Alice's Adventures in Wonderland*, and instead invite ourselves to dive into it, make some magic, and actually create *more* time.

RITUAL   MAKING MORE TIME

The desire to control time has a long lineage. Every spell and enchantment to bestow immortality and every fountain of eternal youth have at their core this longing—to master time. As we remember the magic that is truly our own, we realize that this old desire does not quite hit the mark. Time does not need to be annihilated, dominated, mastered, or overcome for us to have more of it. There is an alternative, a better way. Just as we dote upon the people we love and feel connected to, we might approach time in the same spirit. We cultivate the *right relationship* to time.

This little ritual provides a bit of magic that allows us to do exactly this: to come into deeper relationship with time and, in so doing, to create more for ourselves.

TIME   15 minutes once a day for a 7-day period

MATERIALS
- ~ a stick of incense
- ~ your Making Magic journal
- ~ one of your doors (optional)
- ~ one of your talismans (optional)

PROCESS

Perform the "Easy Breath Relax and Release" found in chapter 2.

If you are working with a door, then you may "open" it in whatever way works best for you at this time—by holding, wearing, noticing, smelling, touching, tasting, for example.

If you are working with a talisman, take a moment to talk to it, sharing with it that your desire for this little ritual is to create a bit more time.

Light your stick of incense. Since an average-sized stick will burn for about ten minutes, it is a very convenient little timekeeper that does its job perfectly well without any bells, alarms, or chimes.

Sitting, standing, or lying down in a position that is comfortable for you, allow yourself to breathe comfortably. There is no right or wrong way to do this; simply bring awareness to your breath and allow that breath over time to slow and deepen. If it doesn't slow and deepen, don't worry about it. You might choose to gently close your eyes, while making sure you do not fall asleep. Feel into the pattern of your breath and no one else's at this moment, into the duration of that stick of incense and no other, and into any other particular sensations, memories, and imaginations. All of these things mark time in different ways and so are different times.

Once you can no longer smell the incense, get up and move around, taking some time to write down any observations or insights in your Making Magic journal. Give special consideration to the question, What is my actual relationship to time?

Do this ritual for seven days, and then go seven more days without doing it. At the end of a two-week period, notice what the quality of your days was like when you took the time to become aware of your breath and gave yourself a little space. Notice what the quality of your days was like when you did not. Did you feel more rushed or pressed for time during one week or the other? What did this ritual teach you about your relationship to time and your ability to take some time for yourself?

FIELD NOTES FROM THE EXTRAORDINARY

If we were to build a clock capable of measuring our deep relationship with time, our sense of extraordinary time, what would it look like? It beggars the imagination in its grandeur and complexity, as well as its naturalness, its simplicity. It would be the most magical of timepieces.

A clock that measures extraordinary time would have to be clock, love letter, and story, all rolled into one, to truly represent our full capacity for the relationship with time that I am suggesting is possible. But it turns out we have exactly such a clock. It is nothing other than the reach and span of our entire lives, our bodies, our minds, and our hearts.

Just as we use tape measures and yardsticks to measure space, we use clocks to measure time. A clock is a *chronometer*, a word that combines *Kronos*, the name of the Greek god of time and father of Zeus, and *meter*, meaning "to measure." Fundamentally, the time measured by our chronometers is a way of measuring periodic motion—in particular, the regular periodic movements of the earth, the sun, and the moon. In this way, there is no arrow of time, no flow of time; that is an idealization and floating abstraction. Our feeling that there is an arrow or flow of time indicates that we are confusing a method of measurement with actual, lived experience.

It is easy to mistake the method of measurement for the phenomenon itself—the periodic movements of our celestial home and our experience "on the ground." The human mind allows itself to be bewitched by ordinary ways of speaking. For example, when we say, "It is nine o'clock!" the *it* is no such thing. Taking back your time means putting those clocks in their rightful place: as mere methods of measurement, not the actual experience we inhabit.

Viewed this way, time becomes less about where we have to be or what we must do at a specific moment according to the clock, and more about telling a story, accounting for an experience, allowing ourselves to pay attention to what we are perceiving, to the movements and the great dance that we are *actually* part of.

This is why in many stories where the everyday and the extraordinary touch, strange things happen to time. It becomes much longer or much shorter. People are gone from their families and communities for only a day, though it felt like a year, or else they are absent for a hundred years, even though it felt like only a night. Time is much more fluid and much less rigid than we might have expected. This is also one of the reasons many traditional cultures that are still in contact with their magic and ceremonies are more flexible about time, often showing up "late" to various events by the dominant cultural standards and also making more time to create and engage in rituals and profound connection with each other.

As you proceed to remember your own magic, it is important to discover and understand the fluidity of time. Magic can be made and worked with to attain specific goals and aims, but as with any practice or any art, some things may take a long time to come together, while others may manifest with lightning speed. We have to let go of the "official" timeline, or the expectation that results must happen always at the same rate or even immediately. Magic-making is not for those who want immediate gratification but for those who want *lasting* gratification—the attainment of which takes its own time. For this reason, while a basic understanding of some traditional magical times can be useful, that usefulness is limited. The whole truth is that while it is always the right time to make magic, there are also different times that you must get attuned to and work with in different ways. Making magic happens in its *own* time and cannot be rushed.

As you discover your own sense of and relationship to time, an awareness of some of the traditionally honored magical times can be of good use.

If you are interested in the sacred art of astrology or simply love star-stories and stargazing, keep in mind that our sense of time is also deeply tied to celestial movements. Consider what celestial bodies and motions you might like to be aware of or more attuned to. Are there planets that you would like to know more about and follow throughout a day, a month, or a year? Are there constellations marking winter or spring that you would like to be able to recognize with your naked eye? Does a calendar that puts as much stock into meteor showers as doctor appointments have deep appeal to you? What celestial events, like equinoxes and solstices, might you want to start noting and setting aside time for?

One of the most beautiful things about the Catholic tradition, practiced by half of my family members, is that every single day in the calendar is a day to honor, remember, and celebrate something. Every day is a feast day, every moment a possibility for embracing the extraordinary within the everyday. Most of the time, these feast days honor specific saints and angels, the stories associated with them, the miracles and magics they performed. A traditional Catholic calendar full of feast days is a tangible reminder to me that there is always time for the sacred.

As you reflect on the questions and prompts above, I encourage you to see the work you are doing and the information you are compiling as the creation of your own personal set of feast days, the days that you choose to set aside for honoring what is sacred and for making magic. Sometimes we resist looking at these questions too closely because we discover that our internal rhythms and preferred sense of time are at odds with our actual daily schedules. While we may not be able to change every aspect of those schedules, awareness is a powerful catalyst for changing the things we can in order to instill within our lives a more extraordinary sense of time.

Once you have gone through the year and made a note of the feast days that you wish to honor and celebrate, create a calendar for yourself that lists them all, and then begin to flesh out each one. What are the celebrations you would attach to it? What prayers and blessings might you say to honor it? What foods would you serve? (Let us always preserve the feast part of feast day!) What rituals might be the best way of honoring and commemorating these times?

The key to tending our time well is to remember that we are ever and always in a relationship with time—a relationship that is or could be reciprocal. This is true in everyday life, but it is also true in making magic. All of the guidelines I have given you above are just this: guidelines. Treat them as the springboards that they are, not bindings or ironclad laws forcing you into certain ways of doing, being in, and thinking about time. We are often told that we can only focus on releasing and letting go of things during a waning moon, or that we can only bless ourselves with the power of the sun on solstice, or that May is the only month we can focus on sweetening our love lives. Some of these times may turn out to be more useful than others, but this terrain of "right" time is too often a rigid area of magic, as magic is commonly understood. Instead, let us understand time correctly: as having been touched by the wild creature that is magic and belonging fully in the domain of our own wild lands.

RITUAL REST TIME

Part of the reason time is so tricky to relate to correctly is we are aware of it only when we are awake. But we spend more than half our life in a state of sleep. Deep, restful sleep is important to us if for no other reason than it provides a feeling of daily renewal and strength—not to mention balance and stability to life and limb. The better our relationship to sleep is, the better our relationship to time can be as well. Sleep and our experience of sleep also uniquely prepare us to experience the shifting fluidity of liminal time.

This ritual will help you assess your relationship with sleep, including and especially the space you inhabit in the everyday as you engage with sleep as a doorway to the extraordinary.

TIME   at least 1 hour

MATERIALS
    ~ your Making Magic journal
    ~ one of your doors (optional)
    ~ one of your talismans (optional)
    ~ an essential oil burner
    ~ a calming essential oil, like lavender or chamomile, or a soothing sacred smoke, like sweetgrass or vanilla leaf (optional)
    ~ a small candle (optional)

PROCESS

Perform the "Easy Breath Relax and Release" found in chapter 2.

If you are working with a door, then you may "open" it in whatever way works best for you at this time—by holding, wearing, noticing, smelling, touching, tasting, for example.

If you are working with a talisman, take a moment to talk to it, sharing with it that your desire for this ritual is to cultivate deeper rest.

So just as you did with your door in chapter 3, look at the space where you sleep. Is it restful? Is the area around your bed free and clear or messy and cluttered? Are there a lot of electronics, with their little lights and beeps and bells, or do you keep your space clear of such devices in order to have better rest? If there are electronic devices around your bed, consider turning them off before you go to sleep.

Consider your bedding. How does it feel against your skin? When is the last time it was washed? Is your pillow supportive and comfortable? Is there anything you need or want when it comes to your bedding that is not present? Is there anything that is present that does not feel necessary?

Also look at the lighting in your space. Darkness has been shown to physiologically promote sleep. Does your space need to be darker? What is the ambient lighting situation? How much ambient light comes in through the windows? If you do feel that your windows need to be darker but can't do anything about that right this minute, then you can use a sleeping mask to help block any ambient light.

Consider your pre-bedtime habits. For maximum clarity and peace of mind as you sleep, it is best not to fall asleep right after watching TV or reading. If you do want to watch TV or read in the evening, try to give yourself a comfortable period of time before you let yourself fall asleep. You get to determine how long that period will be. An hour? Thirty minutes?

Make note of all of your reflections and findings in your Making Magic journal. If you notice certain trends that need to change, then commit to changing them.

Then, when you are ready to go to bed, you may do the following.

First, take a sacred bath. Sacred bathing is a time-honored method of preparing for deep sleep and dreaming, as it will help you remove the psychological detritus of the day. (See chapter 11 for more on sacred bathing.) A favorite sacred bath recipe of mine is one part Epsom salt, one part almond oil, and seven to thirteen drops of lavender essential oil.

If you are not able to fully bathe, you may simply wash your hands and face before sleep as an abbreviated form of sacred bathing.

Signal to yourself that it is bedtime by lighting your small candle, burning some essential oil with a soothing scent like lavender or chamomile, or censing your room lightly with a warm and calming aromatic herb like sweetgrass or vanilla leaf.

After you get into bed, instead of running through the day's events or going over tomorrow's to-do list, try one of these exercises instead.

- Breathe in, and gently bring to mind a specific question you would like to answer. When you breathe out, do so with the intention of letting go something that weighs on you before sleep.

- Bring your mind to the seven directions—north, east, south, west, above, below, and center—not as abstractions, but by fully inhabiting your sensibility of what each direction means for you.

- Reflect on the elements in your body: The warmth of your body is a reflection of fire. Your breath is the element of air. The moisture in your body is water. The weight and heft of your body is the earth. Your singular awareness reflects the soul of the whole world.

Sleep well and dream deeply.

STEPPING STONES

- Think about what your favorite time of day is. Make a point to set aside five minutes to be in that time without anything or anyone distracting you.

- Notice how you wake up. Do you have an alarm clock that makes a terrible sound, or do you get up naturally? If you are unsatisfied with the way that you wake up, then identify why and make whatever changes need to be made.

- Go through a single day without looking at a clock once. See how you feel at the end of the day.

As we explore our inner wilds with greater depth and clarity and sense ourselves growing warmer in our seeking out and remembering of our magic, we may take heart, for we know that we have all of the time that we need, and then some. Time, like our talismans, is yet another place where the everyday is found weaving, dancing, and fully embracing the extraordinary.

Establishing a new relationship to time is another essential part of our journey. And one of the things we shall discover as we come to know time and our ways of connecting to it with more depth and lucidity is that we are decidedly not alone on this journey. We are surrounded by a special sort of kith and kin.

6

KITH AND KIN

You are the result of the love of thousands.

LINDA HOGAN, *Dwellings: A Spiritual History of the Living World*[1]

When we speak of the wild, either literally or metaphorically, we often take it for granted that we are also speaking of the solitary. The words we use to describe actual wild areas in the world—*vast, isolated, remote, far away, far apart,* and *lonely*—imply that our experience in the wild is to be alone. So going into the wild, we assume, means going it alone. And this is doubly so when the terrain we are scouting is that of our own soul, for who can accompany us on our experience as we search out our remembered magic?

However, our ancestors and those who came before us, no matter what culture or people we may belong to, had a strikingly different view of the natural world and all of the places—wild and otherwise—within it. According to their knowing, as accounted for in their stories, songs, images, and reflections, they were never truly alone but were instead surrounded by others at all times. They were held by kith and kin, accompanied by allies, familiars, guides, and guardians—figures that I refer to in my work as holy helpers. This view that was held by people who lived long ago in faraway places the world over can be ours too today, for it speaks directly from our common human experience.

It is the bears who are the holy helpers for Golden Locks. She embarks on a mission to remember magic, and she knows that even though she might seem to be without aid or ally, her experience of reality tells a different story.

In this chapter, we will explore relationships through the notion of our kith and kin. We will begin with the relationships of the everyday, and from our experiences of them, we will learn about what our relationships with and to the extraordinary are, as well as what they can be.

FIELD NOTES FROM THE EVERYDAY

Bring to mind one heart friend. Maybe this person is also a family member, maybe not. But they are beloved by you, a companion who is there whenever you have need. How did you meet? When did your relationship begin? What about them drew you in the first place? What were your early interactions like? When did you know that you were not just going to be casual acquaintances but close friends? What do they love about you? What do you love about them? What have they taught you? How have they helped guide and inspire you? How have they shown up for you through the years? How have you shown up for them?

Reflections on friends and friendships make apparent the reality of and need for reciprocity in relationships or partnerships. A relationship is a dyad—made up of two people. It can have more than two in it, but as it is said often during relationship troubles, "It takes two to tango." If one person wants the other person to flourish and thrive, the first person must be willing to show up for them. Forgiveness is a form of showing up, especially if it is followed by action. Robust and lasting friendships, ones that weather storms, occur when all parties involved make the effort to show up, to say through both word and action, "I care. I am here." Notice that the participants don't follow the path of least resistance. They are willing to show up even for the tough stuff.

The other part of friendship, as a unique form of love, is that it is specific, particular. Your friends are your own friends; there is compatibility between you and your friends. Something very definite, a specific virtue or essence, in your friends draws you to them and to no other in quite the same way.

It is through the friendships and relationships of everyday life that we can learn what right relationship might look and feel like, as well as what relationships require cultivation and tending.

RITUAL IMAGE AND ESSENCE

Sensing out essence and getting a feel for the specific virtue of a person, place, or thing is something that many of us are much more adept at doing than we might think. One of the practical acts that helps us become more skilled at this activity is frequent contact. And we all know that in the business of life, it is easy to lose touch with the people who matter most.

This ritual speaks to this challenge by inviting you to reach out to a specific friend or friends every day for the next seven days. For the purposes of this ritual, I recommend that you call your friend—no emailing or texting—but don't feel pressured to stay on the phone for more than ten minutes.

TIME 10 minutes a day for the next 7 days

MATERIALS
~ your Making Magic journal
~ one of your doors (optional)
~ one of your talismans (optional)
~ a phone

PROCESS

Perform the "Easy Breath Relax and Release" from chapter 2.

If you are working with a door, then you may "open" it in whatever way works best for you at this time—by holding, wearing, noticing, smelling, touching, tasting, for example.

If you are working with a talisman, take a moment to talk to it, sharing with it that your desire for this little ritual is to connect with a beloved and tend that relationship.

Call up a friend to say hello, check on them, see how they are.

After the phone call, make some notes in your Making Magic journal, paying special attention to the question, what quality do I really admire and love in this person, or what qualities do I see as essential to them? Also reflect on how it felt to call them up and what changes you noticed afterward.

Repeat this ritual every day for the next seven days, calling the same friend or different friends each day.

At the end of the week, note in your Making Magic journal how you feel and what you have learned.

The next week proceed as you normally would—either reaching out or not reaching out to your friend(s) as you normally do. What differences do you discover?

FIELD NOTES FROM THE EXTRAORDINARY

From inside the heart of experience, it makes little sense to think that we are alone in our soul's journey. We may climb the tallest mountain, in the remotest part of the world, but the mountain is right there with us, supporting our steep ascent. Even though we may not realize that the mountain is supporting us and our climb, in reality it is. The mountain is simply waiting patiently for us to wake up and realize this fact. After all, it has all the time in the world.

The more we awaken to the relationships that make up our actual experience, the more a specific set of kith and kin that has been with us since time before time comes to light. They are our holy helpers. The word *holy* in this context is not referring necessarily to religious or spiritual figures (though it may) but rather is best understood in relation to its linguistic sisters *whole* and *heal*. Our holy helpers support the creative and magical work of mending the rifts between the worlds of the everyday and the extraordinary, of building the bridges where before there were only chasms.

The first step to getting to know these holy helpers is recognizing the forms they come in. Friends, pets, family members—even and sometimes especially the ones that make us want to stomp our feet in rage and pull out our hair—are all holy helpers. Just as doors can appear in so many ways, and just as talismans can be many things, so our holy helpers can show up in many guises.

Like the wild terrain through which magic lopes, unbound and free, they are around us at all times, no matter where we live or make our homes. They are ravens calling out in raspy voices, encouraging us to laugh at the needed moment. They are rivers dampening our weary toes, cleaning away both dust and sorrow. They are winds whipping the hair out of our tear-filled eyes and confusion away from our ideas. They are the sun, warming the places within us that have been cold for far too long, and the smooth rocks, providing a space to lay it all down and lay it all out.

Then there are the holy helpers who are less familiar or known, more foreign, who ask us to stretch a bit further, to engage the sacred play of the imagination, to play more and feel more deeply. These include our ancestors, the spirits of our beloved dead, and our descendants, those who will come after we are gone. They may include religious figures like gods and goddesses and saints and angels. They include all manner of mythic creature as well. The unicorn, phoenix, dragon, and faerie—like so many figures—are buried under a quaintness that is not part of the genuine insights contained within them. Clear away the sedimentation, get to the shining center, and you will find that each figure contains deep teaching, a particular medicine, its own power or virtue that speaks ever and always to something lasting and completely within our grasp.

Who has not been in touch with the extraordinary and extremely rare at least once? Who has not come through some kind of fire of the soul, or hoarded a certain treasure, or listened to a living wood?

Although we do not talk about our holy helpers with ease, when we begin to pay attention to the possibility of a relationship with them, we often find that they have been following us for years. Reflect on your experience. What plants always seem to be growing near you? What bodies of water and places are you drawn to time and again or find yourself visiting though you scarcely planned to? What is always able to heal your hurting heart or make you laugh? What animals do you know absolutely try to talk with you, and which ones do you best like to talk to? Do you, like many members of my family, collect apparently unremark-able rocks for no clear reason?

In all of the above examples, we see holy helpers that are introducing themselves to us, becoming allies. There may only be one, or there may be many; you may not know how many holy helpers you have at this point. You also may not know for sure whether this being or that being counts as a holy helper, if it really is one or not. It is. It always is.

All we need to do is acknowledge them and begin the work of building real relationships with them. As with any relation-ship, we begin at the beginning, with introductions.

Ask, Who or what is this holy helper? Where is it found? What names does it go by? Who has honored it in the past? Who may honor it now, today? What are its teachings, its medicines, its blessing ways? What is its specific virtue, and how does that connect to your own *telos*? What does your holy helper want you to know or think or do right now? What do you need to do in order to truly care for and tend the relation-ship with your holy helper? What does right relationship with this being look and feel like?

It is through reflecting on questions like this and our experience that the foundation stones for further and deeper relationship are laid down. Allow yourself to play, and see get-ting to know your holy helpers as a kind of creative journey. Be willing to experiment, and be ready to laugh out loud.

Trying to find and work with holy helpers may present some challenges and can be frustrating at first. There has been so much silence and deliberate mystification around this part of magic, and as a consequence, there are few models to work with. The belief that we are alone in the universe, and that the world of nature is devoid of personhood and being, is so deeply held, that it can be difficult to overcome. To work with holy helpers flies in the face of everything we think we know. As it turns out, however, the models are everywhere. An easy place to begin is with the beings you already know and love—your friends, your companions, your beloveds, in all their ways, shapes, and forms.

RITUAL HOLY HELPERS IN THE HOUSE

This little ritual invites you to bring a representation or an icon of one of your holy helpers into your home. Keep in mind that it is not the person or thing that is being honored but your relationship with it. When you honor your relationship with your holy helper, the relationship will become more present for you throughout the day, providing you with a way to tangibly include it in your daily life.

In order to do this ritual, you will need to spend some time playing with the concept of holy helpers and how one might show up for you or make itself known. You will need a physical image of the holy helper you want to honor. This can be an image replicated from your mind and heart, an image reproduced from a dream, a picture that you took or made yourself, a statue or figurine that reminds you of this helper, a written description, or their given (common) name. It can also be a curio representing them—like a feather or a stone or a small vial of water.

TIME   20 to 30 minutes

MATERIALS
- ~ your Making Magic journal
- ~ a physical representation of your holy helper
- ~ a door (optional)
- ~ a special talisman (optional)
- ~ a candle (optional)
- ~ incense (optional)

PROCESS

Perform the "Easy Breath Relax and Release" from chapter 2.

Open your door, share with your talisman your desire for this particular ritual, and light your candles or incense, as you like.

Place the physical representation of your holy helper in front of you so that you can softly focus on it. Allow yourself to gaze at it for a few minutes, just taking it in.

In your Making Magic journal, write a letter to your holy helper. You can introduce yourself or tell them about a specific challenge happening in your life right now. No judgment. It doesn't matter what you write; what matters is that the words come from the heart.

After writing the letter, take a few more minutes to connect with the icon you have selected. Once you have done so, write a response to your letter in your holy helper's voice.

Finally, thank your holy helper, making note of any last impressions in your journal. You may wish to place a clean glass of water in front of their image as well, as clean water is a traditional offering to make to any holy helper with whom you are forming a relationship.

Keep the icon of your holy helper out and visible; if you need to move it to a space where you are more frequently present, do so. Simply being around the physical representation of your holy helper will support your deepening relationship with them. You may find that throughout the day you talk to the image, asking your holy helper questions or seeking out advice, or perhaps you will discover that the image is one that you can study and meditate on for greater clarity.

STEPPING STONES

- Consider what plants or animals seem to always be around you or follow you. Ask yourself if there is a particular plant or animal that shows up for you again and again. Don't be surprised if it seems common. Perhaps white-wing doves seem to follow you wherever you go, or maybe you always bump into African violets. Pay attention to their presence, and when you find yourself wondering if they are holy helpers for you, ask them! My favorite way to do this is to perform the "Easy Breath Relax and Release" and then touch or gaze at the being I am wondering about. Then, in my mind, I will simply ask, "Are you a holy helper for me?" I listen for the response, and I am also open to "hearing" the response in different ways. For instance, it may come through as an image, a poem, a dream, or a song.

- Reflect on the holy helpers that show up consistently in your families of blood and choice. Do you have family or community members with patron saints, special animals, or sacred places that show up again and again? If so, what relationship do *you* have with these saints, animals, or places?

- Notice what beings you pass by every day: the tree in your front yard, the bush by the bus stop. Take a moment to acknowledge their presence and say thank you to them. See what happens next!

"Love is the name for the desire and pursuit of the whole," said the poet Aristophanes.[2] Just as we have friends, companions, and beloveds in the everyday, we also have a tribe of ancestors, guides, guardians, and allies in the world of the extraordinary, ready and waiting for when right relationship makes itself known. Right relationship emerges as we participate more fully in our work of making magic. In other words, you are not alone in this work. You are held.

7

KNOWING NATURE

If we had a keen vision and feeling of all ordinary human life,
it would be like hearing the grass grow
and the squirrel's heart beat, and we should die
of that roar which lies on the other side of silence.
GEORGE ELIOT, *Middlemarch*[1]

Nowhere is the apparent rift between the everyday and the extraordinary more evident than in the most familiar ways the relationship between the human world and the world of nature is regarded. The rift is ultimately rooted in the rift in opinions and beliefs about these two realms. The natural world is full of surprises, and perhaps the greatest is the discovery that nature is everywhere. The common way nature and humans are regarded in belief and opinion does not match up with the reality: the two worlds are, in fact, one world, interpenetrated by diverse and powerful elements—not only physical forces but also holy helpers and native capacities like memory and sacred imagination. Sooner or later the search for magic brings us face to face with a reality beyond the apparent rift between the everyday and the extraordinary, as we explore not only the verdure of our interior life but also our actual relationship with the surrounding world.

Learning how to speak to these holy helpers means learning the language of nature. This is the language of the wild and natural world, the language of the wind through trees and birdsong at dawn. But it is also and equally the language of that wondrous creature called *Homo sapien sapien*, for in knowing nature, we also come to know ourselves.

Golden Locks illustrates this truth in her refusal to buy into the assumed separation between human people and all of the other types of people out there. The common wisdom of her village holds that her people are now utterly separate from the Bear People. Communication is not possible, to say nothing of learning or living side by side. The differences are too great and the similarities too small, if they exist at all. To the villagers, the village is the village, and the forest is the forest, and the divisions between the two are absolute. But Golden Locks doesn't think so, and the offerings that she takes to the Bear People, offerings that came from the forest, symbolize her recognition that the separations between us and them, domestic and wild, man-made and natural, are mere words that often disintegrate in the face of reality. Magic reminds us that full, intact, and complete self-knowledge is contiguous with knowledge of the whole, of all of Creation.

All magic originates in the natural world. From the ingredients used in ritual and ceremony, to the clothing worn, the talismans treasured, the foods eaten, and the medicines taken—all of them begin among plant and fungi, animal and mineral, as do we. The role that nature plays in magic cannot be overstated, but it can be misunderstood. Magic is like a wild animal, but in the common understanding, what *wild* actually means tends to be a pale and shadowy reflection of what it really *is*.

This chapter is an opportunity to stretch out that understanding, to fatten it up, give it glossy fur and claws that mean business. The starting point is to consider what a daily relationship to the natural world could look like and where it tends to take place. From there, you can explore the ways you might deepen that relationship, to find the extraordinary within it and enlist the aid of nature in making magic.

FIELD NOTES FROM THE EVERYDAY

The experience of nature does not begin in a wild forest or rushing river valley. It begins right here. If we cannot discover the materials we need for magic already present in the everyday, then we will not find them at all, no matter how far we journey, no matter how breathtaking the scenery along the way. Noticing is a lifetime of work. For most of us, noticing will not happen in a pure and unpolluted wild place, for these places are few and far between and often hold secrets that are not meant for us. It will instead happen in our kitchens and front yards, where nature is just as present.

What is entirely familiar and known, hidden in plain sight? Where might nature be found? One answer is, the kitchen and the cupboard. These are the spaces where nature has made herself most at home *within the home itself.* In folk traditions, magic was made in the kitchen—through cooking and making use of the ingredients found within the kitchen, from the spice cabinet to the pantry, and since the advent of the icebox and refrigeration, the fridge. For it is here in the kitchen, even within the simplest and most stripped-down kitchen, that we routinely come into contact with some of the most tangible elements of the natural world—animals, plants, minerals, earth and air, fire and water.

Go into your kitchen and pick one area: the spice drawer, the cupboard, your refrigerator. Pull everything out and set it on the counter. What comes from animals? What comes from plants? From fungi and bacteria? From minerals? Don't limit this inquiry. Glass is formed from silica and fire. Plastic is a petroleum by-product, and what is petroleum but a product mined from the earth? Paper wrappings started off as trees. Metal appliances were once veins of ore buried within the dark ground. Dare to find one item that did not begin its life firmly rooted in nature; it is not possible. You needn't go into a nature preserve to come into contact with the whiskers and muddy paw prints of magic. There it is, padding across the stovetop and through the pantry.

As you go through the above process in your kitchen, certain ingredients will stand out above all the others. They seem to have vibrancy, an attraction. They feel potent. As a root doctor or cunning woman might say, they have mojo.

When it comes to working, wandering, *and* wondering through the wilds of the kitchen, it is important to heed your own personal responses and impressions, and not be overly concerned with conforming your taste to dictionaries and lists of correspondences compiled by various sources. Meanings and interpretations are best grown from the soil of your direct experience; these are the meanings and interpretations that are *just right*.

A sacred artist who knows ten different ways to work with a single ingredient will make more effective magic than one who has the wherewithal to buy ten different exotic ingredients. Why? Because in the former case, there is real relationship. In the latter, there is merely acquisition, and they are not the same. So start where you are and with what you have.

RITUAL KITCHEN MAGIC

In response to the increasing tempo of modern life, many wonderful grocery stores offer prepared foods as a convenience. When cooking is outsourced regularly, however, we become detached from the necessities of food preparation, from the ingredients of the food, from the nature of the food, as well as from the space or nexus that holds the cooking and food in the home. We lose a sense of the alchemy inherent in all of these things. So, given this newfound knowledge based on our own experience and a desire to explore kitchen magic a little further, it is time to cook something up!

This ritual is not about releasing the inner Julia Child (although if you feel called to do so, then by all means do). It is about taking time to connect with nature hidden in plain sight, in your own dwelling space, and coming to know one aspect of it as well as possible.

TIME   1 hour

MATERIALS
- ~ a simple recipe
- ~ your Making Magic journal
- ~ a door (optional)
- ~ a special talisman (optional)
- ~ a candle (optional)
- ~ incense (optional)

PROCESS

Perform the "Easy Breath Relax and Release" from chapter 2.

Open the door; touch your talisman, sharing with it your desire for this ritual; and light the candle or incense, as you like.

Begin to prepare the recipe. Take time for and give attention to each step. Pause and feel into the ingredients you are working with—where they came from, how they arrived in your home. Even boiling spaghetti in water can become a springboard. The spaghetti was once wheat, in a field—where? What did its life cycle look like? What animals and plants depended on it?

Record your impressions in your Making Magic journal.

Make the serving and eating of the food a ritual as well, allowing yourself to fully savor the entire experience. When you are attentive and open to what the ingredients actually feel and taste like—and not just the idea you have of them—you discover their essence or inherent properties, qualities that can't be taken away. Be open and curious about the differences that make garlic *garlic* or an apple *apple*.

FIELD NOTES FROM THE EXTRAORDINARY

As we recollect our magic, many ideas and notions that we uncover might sound far out and radical at first. Doors are magical. Time can be bent, expanded, and collapsed. Holy helpers have always been present, if not seen. Inanimate objects sing to our souls. The extraordinary not only exists but also is available here and now if we are willing to look. Any one of these ideas would make a skeptic smile wryly and laugh out loud, but nothing is as radically transformed and pushed to the edges by remembering our magic as our relationship with the natural world. The view of a world that is ensouled, animate, unfolding in dynamic relationships, and possessing essence changes us from the inside out.

From the kitchen, we move outside. Look at your front or backyard; look at the city sidewalk or stoop of stairs. What lives there? What is growing there? What is wild in these places? Silver moonlight trails of slugs, tough city birds with greasy wings and missing toes and bright eyes nonetheless, plantain weeds, and those dandelions that seem able to grow out of sheer concrete and asphalt—each one is a potential teacher, an ally, and an inspiration for making magic.

If you don't have a yard or a garden, then go and find one—a city park or a community garden. What is growing and living and breathing in these spaces? Most likely you will discover that you know only a few of their names. Do as any good magician would and learn the proper names, because names matter. Learn their stories and life ways. What knowledge and teachings do they hold? What kind of magic might they be *just right* for making?

Do not be surprised when everything becomes a person, with its own *telos*, no matter how different from our own. You will walk away from each exploration with an ever-longer list of magical allies and ingredients, learnings and teachings, and it will take more than a lifetime to learn to work with them all.

RITUAL GETTING IT JUST RIGHT

This ritual supports you in moving from a comprehensive view of the natural elements to a more specific framework by focusing on a single purpose and then pairing it with a single ingredient.

TIME 15 to 30 minutes

MATERIALS

~ a kitchen, a garden, a backyard, or a set of front steps

~ your Making Magic journal

PROCESS

Perform the "Easy Breath Relax and Release" from chapter 2.

Think about one concrete situation that you would like to transform with magic. Maybe there is a work situation that needs changing, or a partnership that needs to be sweetened, or a hurt that needs to be healed. In your Making Magic journal, briefly describe the situation and then write out what you would like to accomplish.

Now, standing in your kitchen/garden/backyard/front steps, allow yourself to feel into the space as you hold the situation and the goals for it in your mind, heart, and body.

What ingredient or element shows up for you as you feel into the space? Start with just one.

When you have it, sit down with it, much as you did with the icon of your holy helper. What impressions does it give? How might these be incorporated into a ritual?

There are no right or wrong answers. Let yourself play, explore, dream, and imagine. Write down your observations and ideas.

When you are ready, breathe in a blessing on yourself and the ingredient that showed up for you. Exhale in gratitude.

Final step: create the ritual you described, perform it, and note how effective it is.

STEPPING STONES

- Buy yourself a bouquet of flowers or go gather some outside. Take time to really look at them and inhale their fragrance. Which ones speak to you the most profoundly?

- Don't have time at the moment to cook? No worries. Go out to dinner at your favorite restaurant. Give yourself time to truly savor the meal, indulging in all of its different tastes, scents, and textures. Notice if any one part or ingredient of the meal stands out for you. If so, consider where else you have come across it in your life.

- Pretend you are a god or goddess. What offerings would you most like to have left on your altar? Your answers will give you excellent insight into what some of your favorite ingredients might be to work with in a magical setting.

We acquire self-knowledge through patient observation and an intimate knowledge of nature. Conversely, we know nature through patient self-reflection and understanding. Observation based on our own experience, coupled with self-reflection, is a vital step in remembering magic. This remembering, in turn, gives us another gift, that of finding ways to feel truly at home in the world. For even a creature as wild as magic is in need of shelter, of hearth and home.

8

HEARTH AND HOME

The territory of everyday experience indicated in this book thus far and the activities of seeking, remembering, imagining, relating, encountering, honoring, and creating provide the necessary conditions for making magic that is our own. Just as magic possesses both inner and outer qualities, so do the everyday experiences of life. So it is not surprising that the further we venture into unmarked inner territories, the more we are compelled to honor that journey and our many discoveries in a variety of outer, external spaces. We can create a place or a space that frees the play of our inmost thoughts, feelings, and magic-making potential. Spaces that honor the interiority—not just of the soul in the abstract but also of your soul in particular—are among the most precious and needful things in life.

As our journey continues, we come to find that magic is not only present in the natural world around us; it has also taken up residence right beside us in our homes. The official story we often hear is that magic is only found in wild nature, but this idea is simply another way to attempt to fence in magic. The true story is that magic refuses to be fenced in, and so it pops up anywhere we are, including in the supposedly least wild places of all: our hearths, our homes. Discovering the presence of magic for yourself even in domestic life, you will find that the making and crafting of home spills over effortlessly into the joy of creating beautiful and blessed altars. We see that there is a deep and necessary connection between making our own homes in the world and the making of altars.

Altars are sacred places that are consulted for inspiration and instruction. Golden Locks' tasks in the bears' cave were all centered around building altars. Her challenge was to find the way to get each altar *just right*, and she succeeded not by accepting preformed possibilities but rather by creating her own spaces, bringing objects together in her own way, making the choices that enabled her to make something entirely unique to her. It is the same for us. We cannot create an altar from a recipe or a book, not really. Our altar-building, like our home-building and our magic, must come from within.

The home is one of the primary places where magic resides. This chapter is an invitation to explore this territory with keen eyes and sharpened senses. You will again discover that what you seek is close at hand, as you open the magical potential of dwellings and create specific spaces for more vivid and concentrated encounters with the wild creature called magic. In the process, you will find that altars are the original crossroads where spirit and matter, the sacred and the profane, immanent and transcendent, and everyday and extraordinary are able to meet up and make themselves at home.

FIELD NOTES FROM THE EVERYDAY

In the most basic way, a house provides shelter for the body. Usually we say that shelter is a necessary condition for body's well-being. And there is truth to this. But magic invites us to look at the *other* side. The body is a necessary condition for shelter. For our bodily existence is *prior* to any dwelling we happen to find or to build; any dwelling place presupposes that we have bodily existence with which to dwell. For this reason, there is perhaps no better place to begin in the everyday than with the living organism of the human body—*your* body.

Your body's form is itself a place, a very specific place in the cosmos, and is not at all the abstract "matter" we sometimes confuse it with. At its healthiest and most flourishing, body is a cosmic outlaw, a law-breaker, resisting the law of entropy and refusing to be ground to dust. There is nowhere or nothing on earth exactly like your own body; it is the unique place in which your unique and beautiful heart resides. How you relate to and care for your living body directly correlates with the way that you experience issues not only of heart and soul but also of space and form, all potential houses and homes, all possible altars and sacred spaces. Everything flows from this one point. Knowing this inaugurates a sea change in our lives.

Being wounded, hurt, or suffering is not just about being in a state of discomfort. The essence you carry within and the *telos* to which your life speaks are imperiled as well. When a precious body is damaged and killed, it is not just the harm or loss of life that is mourned; it is the loss of one more place where the sacred found a home and now cannot. It is a loss that leaves no one, not even the most callous among us, untouched. Likewise, when we cherish, care for, celebrate, and honor our living bodies—in all their sizes and shapes, forms and colors—when we *adore* and *adorn* them, then they are strong and resilient places through which we may commune and connect with all that is sacred and most meaningful. (Note that *adore* and *adorn* are both cognates of the word *altar*.)

Magic encourages us to look not only to the way we cherish and care for our own bodies in the everyday but also to the way we cherish and adore other people's bodies in many life-affirming and healing ways. Remember our work with right relationship from the previous chapter. A mother cherishes the body of her baby; a lover cherishes the body of their beloved. A chef with a vision for tasty and wholesome food that comes from farm to table, or a woman building a farmers' market that honors quality and fairness, indeed cares for the body's life. The owner and creator of a belly-dance studio and program for teen women has a vision for building a dance culture that supports the glorious movements of the beautiful body in a way that encourages dignity and respect. We have sovereignty over our bodies. But we are not alone, not even in our bodies. Bodily relationship forms the basis or the ground of all of our most everyday experiences, from the most practical experiences to our most cherished and sacred relationships to others.

Because of the body's existential priority, home could never be just where we live, hang our hats, or go to bed at night. Home is not in the dwelling spaces we build and create—with wood, brick, stone, mortar, and glass. Home is literally where the heart is. A magical way of looking at a house is to see it working like a sacred icon of the heart—an icon pointing to the very source of our sense of home, the heart. Just as sacred icons or images on holy altars serve to draw lines of convergence with a sacred reality, our dwelling spaces can help to draw lines of convergence to the immanent center of the heart. And they can do so powerfully, to the extent that our familiar houses create a convincing illusion: that the place we return to at the end of every day *is* home. But because the body is the body, and the soul is the soul, we find that each of us is capable of inhabiting many dwelling spaces that all serve to remind us of the heart. It is possible, then, to feel at home in more than one place and indeed in many different places.

Ordinarily, those of us living in the modern world will go about our business without noticing where we live. All too often, we notice where we live only when a problem arises in the structure of our house. Something needs to be fixed. We call the plumber because the pipes are clogged, or we call the electrician because the light switch fails. It is easy to take these problems and our dwelling places for granted. It's also easy to take for granted those holy helpers who come to the aid of the concerned householder. The true meaning of our dwellings—the protection and nurture they offer us—is hidden in plain sight, as is the meaning of the surroundings and relationships that form the living context of all dwellings.

What does the word *home* actually mean? What does it mean to feel at home? To be at home is to be able "to let our hair down" and "come off it" and feel free of being under pressure to be something we are not. When we are "at home," we know that here, in this space more than in any other, we can at long last be ourselves. Home is a space where unfolding, opening, and expanding happen. It is also a space where rest, relaxation, and succor take place. Home possesses the power of calling us forth into the truth, into a level of authenticity not found anywhere else. This authenticity is nothing we have to make up or contrive. It is in the home most of all that we might hope to be fully honest with ourselves and others—honest in artless simplicity and directness.

A home is a special place, and we all have special places that we find or build or create for ourselves within our homes and outside our homes. What are those places in your life?

Like treasure and talisman gathering, forming or discovering these places begins in childhood. Whether your taste runs to the simple and clean or to the elaborate and extravagant, or somewhere in between, creating little spaces that are just your own is something you already do in your own way.

Consider leaves that we bring home from the playground and nestle in between rocks and toys, and twigs on our top shelves, and desks that create a language that, while inscrutable to grown-ups, makes perfect sense to children. What is the character and spirit of the *space* that these things create? We never outgrow the habit of creating spaces for ourselves that reflect ourselves. Office desks do not need pictures of friends and family or spider plants in order to function as desks, and bedside tables do not require piles of dog-eared books, pens, and fat candles in order to perform their duties. Mantles are not waiting for icons of holy helpers to be placed on them just so, and dining room tables can be put to use whether there are pretty cloths on them or not. And yet knowing all of this will not stop us from bringing a picture of a beloved pet to work, adding another book to the bedside table, feeling an unnamed longing when we spy a starkly naked mantle, or snapping a cherry-red cloth over the dining room table to herald the coming of summer.

Continue your reflections. Where do you locate home? What does home mean to you? What does a place need in order for it to feel like home for you? What is not needed for you to feel at home? Have you ever had the experience of living in a place but not feeling like it was home? What objects, scents, colors, smells, and spaces signify home to you? What makes you comfortable? What helps you relax? What leaves you feeling safe and secure? What inspires you? What needs to be in place in order for you to be able to rest? What homes have you visited that resonated with you? (Remember that we can take *home* in these questions in a broad sense; it does not just have to mean "house.") What homes have you visited that felt "off" somehow? Why did they feel that way? Who needs to be present for you to feel at home?

Watch a dog or a cat. They will claim a spot—a kennel if they have one, or a chair, or a part of the bed—as their own. It becomes their den, and if we leave our pet unattended, we find that they bring bits of this and bobs of that to their special place. Observe a bird building its nest. Why that twig and not the other? Why this piece of red yarn but not that piece of turquoise silk? Our fellow creatures may not choose in the same way we do, but they still exercise choice and deliberation in their creations. A home is being prepared and made for the precious treasure of life; a place of one's own, where something of one's authentic nature and experience blossoms into fullness and comes into the light, is being created.

We already possess ample experience in transforming the elements of a house into a home, and thus we are capable of discovering hitherto undreamt-of magical potential, right under our noses.

RITUAL HOME BODY

Homes are not only like icons of the heart; they are also mirrors: in hundreds of big and small ways, they reflect who we are into the spaces we occupy.

Mirrors have a long history of use in magic. They are used to create illusions, to tell the future, to seduce and beguile, and to reflect. A long-understood magical precept is that whatever we see reflected in a mirror depends on what we bring to the mirror. So it is that if we come before a mirror with hearts that are afraid or hurting, we see things that make us afraid and can hurt us. If we approach a mirror with courage or love, then we may spy the ones we love, the ones who love us, the battles we shall win or lose, with grace. In many stories, the trick to working with a mirror successfully is approaching one with the desire to see and discover what is actually there—what actually needs to be seen.

This is a ritual that speaks to the potency of mirrors and what we may find within them.

TIME 15 to 20 minutes

MATERIALS
- ~ candles
- ~ a full-length mirror
- ~ your Making Magic journal
- ~ a door (optional)
- ~ a special talisman (optional)
- ~ incense (optional)

PROCESS

Perform the "Easy Breath Relax and Release" from chapter 2. Open your door; or touch your talisman, sharing with it your desire for this ritual; and light your incense, as you like.

Place your candles on either side of the mirror so that they form a gateway. Light the candles.

Make sure that the artificial lights in the room are off. Or if you must have them on, make them as dim as possible.

Stand naked in front of the full-length mirror. Notice the play of light and shadow over your skin, muscles, fat, curves, rolls, and ripples.

As you gaze at your body, your first altar, allow yourself to imagine what would change in your life if you saw your body as a place, a home, to express adoration for. How would you express adoration for it? How can you best honor the altar that is your blessed body?

What does your experience of the mirror through which you see yourself and your body tell you about your relationship to altars?

Record your findings in your Making Magic journal.

※

A beautiful way to follow up this little ritual is with either a sacred bath (see chapter 11) or the "Body Blessing" ritual in chapter 10.

FIELD NOTES FROM THE EXTRAORDINARY

As we look deeply at the sense of home, we uncover the same wild terrain in which magic is found. Already, in the process of finding and making our homes, we have formed an altar, or the rudiments of an altar, without realizing it. Making home—an image of the heart—turns out to be one way we can make magic. When the wild creature that is magic stalks through territory that is our true home ground and home turf, we know it. It shows up in our ability to be straight with ourselves. By intuition and instinct, in exactly the same way that geese know when and how to fly south for the winter and north for the summer, we know that *this* is where we belong—the specific activities, places, and people that help us remember distinctly and in no uncertain terms our deepest center. The magic of home also shows up as a willingness to fight and protect what is our own—the lands, domiciles, terrains, and sacred places. But the imprints left by the wild creature that is magic are often subtle, and it is easy to lose track of a true sense of home, a true sense of self.

Every moment grants us the gift of the potential to make and find home. Every occasion is one in which an altar may be revealed. Like everything else our remembered magic has brought our attention to, we will be surprised by what we discover. Go through your home right now, looking closely and carefully, and you will find them in places you might never have expected. The way that your perfume bottles are arranged, or the place where you kick off your shoes upon first coming inside, or the front door and the items placed beside it. Could it be that the mess in your closet or junk drawer is a little altar, however unconsciously created on your part, honoring a desire you have for freedom, marking your relationship to what is out of your control? The paintings hung on walls and the places to bathe and pray and make love—each one, an altar.

As we find and create our altars, our homes for the sacred, we may find ourselves wondering, what do we do with them? Just as you had to look to your own inner knowing for creating your altars, you also look to it for inspiration on how to work with each altar. Carpenters have workbenches and work spaces. An altar is a work space for seeking out and making magic.

In the last chapter, you were invited to think about what kind of specific situation(s) could be addressed magically, and that question applies here as well. Do you want to be able to make magic at your altar? If so, what ingredients, tools, and items might you need? Incense? Candles? A sharp knife to cut through nonsense? Pens? Papers? Silly Putty? The rocks you found at the shoreline? Do you want to be able to offer up prayers and petitions at your altar? What needs to be in place for that work?

Like the art maker, the magic maker gets to decide what direction to take the work and the work space. But at bottom, we never forget that the creative play of the sacred imagination at work with altars is something ultimately we do for the sake of itself, for the inherent richness of the experience—like dancing the night away, making love, having great feasts of merriment and joy, or enjoying heart-to-heart conversations.

For people whose life partners do not understand or approve of remembered magic, the space best for magical work may be the shower or bathtub, or even in a portable shrine that can be carried from place to place. The shrine need not be physical but can be located within the space of the sacred imagination.

Altars do not have to be permanent or elaborate; they do not need to be inside the house, nor do they need to have anything on them. The best altar might be the knoll under a cottonwood tree or the side of a dusty hill where you can park your car and look up at the stars.

When creating your altars, consider any animals and young children who may be in your home. Cats and toddlers especially can be wonderful collaborators when creating altars, but they also can be forces of destruction. Children who are interested in altar spaces might be given assistance in creating their own altars where they may play, dream, and create. Each space can be respected and cared for, and in this way, the meaningful work of remembered magic is carried forward into the next generation.

Like other areas of magic, the creation and construction of altars is one that might seem to have a lot of rules. You might easily form this idea from books on the subject or especially from popular entertainment. They say an altar must be facing a certain direction or only be worked with at dawn, or dusk, or high noon. It must have these five essential tools on it and is not a "real" altar unless it is at least this tall. And on and on it goes. This is another case where too many rituals and ceremonies have the mark of endless labyrinths that lead nowhere, or like Ptolemy's "epicycles," they seem to needlessly compound all sorts of arcane movements and prescriptions.

We are more Copernican in our direction, exercising Occam's razor. Given a choice to walk through the elaborate labyrinthine rituals or to go straight for the holy mountain, we go straight for the mountain. Magic, like all wild things, does not accept or settle into assumed roles, nor does it follow impatient demands. It goes its own way, making its home in all places where the everyday and extraordinary are woven together. We do well to keep this in mind when creating altars (or acknowledging the spaces already created that truly are altars).

There are no rules for making an altar, just as there are no rules for making a home. But there are things that work and things that will not work. No one can tell you how to make your altar. Your doors and talismans, your knowledge of the times that are meant to be attended and honored, your relationships to holy helpers, your innate knowing of nature—these are the things that inform the creation of true altars. These are the places where inspiration and instruction can be found. This approach makes the altar truly your *own*, strong and able to sing.

RITUAL ESTABLISHING YOUR ALTAR

No single ritual can tell us how to make an altar, and the needs around altars change from time to time. Here, then, is a basic outline for establishing the space for any altar you might feel called to create. You may use this ceremony whenever you need to make or build, or remake or rebuild, an altar. It calls on basic ingredients, most of which you should be able to find in your kitchen.

TIME   30 to 60 minutes

MATERIALS

- ~ your Making Magic journal
- ~ Kosher salt
- ~ oil—a ritual anointing oil for a general purpose like blessing or purification, or a plain olive or almond oil
- ~ 2 glasses of water, whether natural spring water, water that you have blessed or water that has been blessed by someone else, as you like
- ~ an herb that you can light and cense over the altar— good choices include pine, juniper, bay leaf, palo santo, or white sage (any aromatic herb will do)
- ~ a door (optional)
- ~ a special talisman (optional)
- ~ a candle (optional)
- ~ incense (optional)

PROCESS

Perform the "Easy Breath Relax and Release" from chapter 2. Open your door; touch your talisman, sharing with it your desire for this ritual; and light your candles or incense, as you like.

Affirm and acknowledge that you are going to designate your chosen space to be your altar.

Breathe in a blessing on the space and exhale in gratitude.

Place a small pinch of salt on the space where the altar will be created. Request aloud that any inner or outer resistance to your ability to remember your magic and create a sacred space be rendered null and void by the salt. You may say something along these lines: "May I remember my magic wholly and completely, and may any impediment to remembering be rendered null and void." Or you may use your own words.

Sweep the salt up and pour it into one of the glasses of water. As it dissolves, affirm and acknowledge that, at the same time, it dissolves all resistance, inner and outer, to the work at hand.

Breathe in another blessing on the space and exhale in gratitude.

Request aloud that all good blessings and benefits that are present in this space be blessed with life and vitality now as you cleanse the space and make room for them. You may say something along these lines: "May all who enter and come into contact with this space be blessed and a blessing in turn." Or you may use your own words.

Sprinkle the space with the water from the second glass (the glass that you did not add the salt to). If there is any water left in that glass, pour it into the ground or a potted plant, or save it to offer to a living plant later.

Breathe in another blessing on the space and exhale in gratitude.

Request aloud that all who enter and work in this space be blessed and protected. You may say something along these lines: "May all who enter and come into contact with this space come in love and depart in peace." Or you may use your own words.

Anoint the space with the oil. If you are working with a quadrilateral, putting a slight dab at each of the four corners and at the middle of the space is traditional. If you are working with a differently shaped space, then a tiny dab of oil wherever you feel called to make it is just fine.

Affirm and acknowledge that the space has been sealed in blessing and protection.

Breathe in another blessing on the space and exhale in gratitude.

Light the aromatic herb and allow the smoke to drift over the space.

As you are ready, allow yourself to simply be in the space, feeling into it, listening, and paying attention.

Note any strong impressions in your Making Magic journal.

Final act: begin the process of building your altar. Once you have completed it, breathe in a final blessing on yourself and the space you have created, and exhale in gratitude. Then the next day, begin working with your altar in whatever ways are best for you.

STEPPING STONES

- Go to a place in nature that feels sacred and special to you, acknowledging it as an altar space. Stay there for a while and notice how you feel when you are in that space. Some of those sensations are ones you will want to invite in when you are ready to build your own altar.

- Take a quick survey of your home, asking yourself if you have been building altars all along without even knowing it. If so, identify where they are and what purposes they serve. What does their presence tell you about your areas of focus and emphasis?

- Let yourself imagine what your ideal altar space would look like. As we did in chapter 2, create a collage or use a virtual collaging program to add to this space elements that speak to you. Then once you are ready to create your own altar, you will be that much more prepared!

Within magical traditions, the crossroads is a highly regarded symbol and physical location, viewed as a doorway, a liminal threshold, and a concrete example of how the everyday and extraordinary weave themselves together and into one another. The crossroads is another kind of sacred center. Take heed how the idea of the crossroads is held: as in everything else, what is needed for magic-tracking is closer than we think. There is no internal necessity that says we must drive miles away from home in order to find a crossroads and to experience the meeting of everyday and extraordinary. In truth, we are surrounded by such interstices, for they dot every part of our living terrain. The altars created, rebuilt, and rediscovered are only some examples of these primary meeting places. They are the crossroads that surround and interpenetrate human life at all times. And although crossroads at first blush seem to be the opposite of home, as sacred centers, they in fact help make home manifest. It is there, at those "altars," that we stand firm in both worlds, rooted in the wild-soul soil, remembering magic, weaving the worlds together once more. From that position, we are then ready to proceed along the next step of the journey, one of call and response.

9

CALL AND RESPONSE

Dreams are the guiding words of the soul. Why should I henceforth not love my dreams and not make their riddling images into objects of my daily consideration?

CARL JUNG, *The Red Book* (John Peck and Mark Kyburz, translators)[1]

Night has fallen. It is very dark this evening, for it is a new moon. You are sitting on your favorite swing under a tree, rocking and listening. All is encircled in stillness and quiet. There is not much going on that you can see, yet the quiet that surrounds you is somehow full of life. You are experiencing the quiet as an empty fullness, as paradoxical as that might sound. But that's the way the quiet is in our experience. Just as the wild places within day-to-day life and the world are not solitary, the silences we actually experience in the wild are not vacuous, dead silences. The quiet we experience is a living silence, not characterized by a total absence but rather by living presence—a living presence that is, in fact, defined by relationship.

Consider the countless unseen relationships that weave together to make the feeling of being present and alive. First, there are relationships in your own body and your breath. But then move out from there. The air is cool and clear. The rope of the swing strains with the tension of your weight and movement. Wind sighs through branches in the tree above. The bedrock has been moving slowly for eons under tremendous pressure, but for you, right now, the ground supports you and everything else nearby. Earthworms wriggle down deep into the soil, spiders spin out their silken webs, elk bugle to each other across vast calderas under the night sky, and coyotes perform forgotten rituals in the high hills. All are present whether any can be heard or not. And all are performing their movements together like a dance or like ocean currents. The encircling quiet we experience is full of the indications of a deeper movement out of sight and beyond our hearing. The sighs, shufflings, snaps, crunches, and little peeps are like the crests of breaking waves or ripples on the surface of water, of some much larger reality that we are part of, a reality that sings and winks to us: *relationship*.

Nothing exists outside relationship. The presence you feel presupposes deep relationship at work. And the most primary relationship at work is between your own soul and the world.

As it weaves itself between the worlds of the everyday and the extraordinary, remembered magic calls to us in quiet ways throughout our lives, and at some point, we hear or feel the call clearly enough that it triggers a process of recollection, an unveiling of a much deeper reality that reminds us of our relationship to it, reminds us of what it means to be magical, what it means to seek out and be in possession of our own magic. Like the woven worlds of the everyday and extraordinary, the structure of being is reciprocal, one of call and response woven tightly together.

As we go deeper into Memory, the mother of the Muses, seeking out magic, an attunement to the dance of call and response through the sacred arts of dream and divination takes place. It is through her dreams that Golden Locks finds the courage to go off into the forest in search of her beloved Bear People and the magic that they have kept. Dreams, especially sequences of dreams or recurring dreams, show up in many stories and myths, from the *Iliad* and the *Odyssey* to the Rig Veda of Hinduism to the Jewish Tanakh, all the way down to tales like "Beauty and the Beast" and "Donkeyskin" and faerie lore, including Shakespeare's *A Midsummer Night's Dream*. In each case, the dreams point the way to matters of a pressing nature in the everyday world. As we shall see, dreams are a specific form of divination.

We are walking much closer to magic now than ever before. Its presence is everywhere. Its scent grows sharper, stronger. Its breath is closer to our skin as the worlds begin their weaving. Its voice can be heard, as if in the sound of distant music. Throughout this chapter, we shall be attending to and heeding that voice, listening for its call, listening to its response, learning how to make calls and responses of our own through the two sacred arts of dreams and divination.

FIELD NOTES FROM THE EVERYDAY

Our everyday experience is built around the structure of call and response. Who except a hermit can go through one day without receiving phone calls, emails, text messages, or even handwritten cards and letters? Chances are, someone is calling now, trying to get in touch with you. Probably at some point you will need to put this book down to take a call, send a text, answer an email.

Within this everyday reaching out to each other nestles something very special. Consider all the ways that we—friends and strangers and even enemies—reach out to each other. Sometimes we are just getting in touch to say hello. Other times we may have specific information that we need to receive or give. Occasionally we may send a warning, a silly joke to make a person laugh, or a clear set of instructions pertaining to a given situation.

Each one of these forms of communication is a call, and typically they are responded to in kind. Not responding is itself a response—as every heart-stricken lover knows. Responses themselves then turn into calls. From asking friends if they want to meet up for coffee or a drink, to getting a significant other to go out for a night on the town, to calling the insurance company in order to wrangle and negotiate an unfair bill—our lives are shaped and given definition by the calls we send out and the responses to those calls, just as our lives are defined by our relationships with kith and kin.

Being called may be spoken of in a less everyday manner, as when someone feels called to join or to leave a specific faith tradition, to go back to school, to move to a different place, to begin a new project, or to begin taking on a particular set of practices. In all cases, our ability to call out for what we desire and need, as well as our ability to respond to the calls we receive with wisdom, discernment, and effective actions, is dependent upon our willingness to listen, to pay attention, *and* to articulate clearly what our true goals and desires really are.

Reflection on the experience of call and response at play in everyday life discloses a variety of preferences as to the way call and response takes place. Feel into this for a moment. What calls do you find yourself happiest to respond to? Do you look forward to social calls but loathe the idea of calls reminding you of certain obligations? Do party invites stress you out, while you are all too happy to respond to workplace requests? What calls are the ones you would rather ignore altogether and not deal with? What kinds of response do you love to give? Is it easy to say yes and difficult to say no or vice versa? Do you feel that when you give a response that is perhaps not what the other person was looking for, you have to justify or explain yourself unduly? Do you like giving a one-line response that takes a few seconds to send out, or do you prefer taking your time and issuing a thoughtfully crafted reply?

Along these same lines, think about what forms of call and response work best for you. Do you enjoy emailing people over texting them? Does the idea of making a phone call make you want to hide your head under a pillow? Do you wish that all mail were delivered on beautiful paper and all words written with a good pen?

"Know thyself," the Delphic Oracle says, and for us, that is an injunction to find a knowing that issues from our own actual living experience. For it is exactly here, in the experience of the everyday, that we begin to remember magic. When we remember magic, patterns around such things like call and response carry far greater significance and depth than we will have perhaps realized. As in other areas of the everyday, relationship to the extraordinary is quite conditioned by relationship to the everyday. If there are problems here, there will certainly be problems there.

We will find that overtly exclusive ideas around call and response begin to disintegrate in the face of lived experience. Responding to an email is often a relatively straightforward affair. Witnessing an injustice, feeling called to do something about it, and then responding in the form of writing, art, sculpting, dance, song, or music—that is less straightforward. In such situations, certain people are willing to risk more, to let themselves be seen, to respond with as much truth as they possibly can. This kind of a call and response often leaves a mark on us, leaves us feeling a little raw and bruised, but also exceedingly clear and confident in where we stand. In this way, call and response is a refining experience; it changes the soul. The more deeply a call is heard, the more honest are the responses. And with greater honesty in thought and life, sovereignty grows, right where we stand. What we are willing to fight for, what we really want, and how to best honor our deepest sense of purpose, our *telos*, all becomes clarified.

RITUAL GIVE ME A SIGN

This is a ritual that I often give to my students and clients when they want to know if a specific prayer, request, or ritual is going to successfully support them in their endeavors or not. It is one that I was taught within my own family but also have had reinforced by my beloved elderly clients, who also grew up in traditions where magic was more overtly present and honored. It is the essence of simplicity.

TIME   15 to 20 minutes

MATERIALS
- ~ your Making Magic journal
- ~ a door (optional)
- ~ a special talisman (optional)
- ~ candles (optional)
- ~ incense (optional)

PROCESS

Perform the "Easy Breath Relax and Release" from chapter 2. Open your door; touch your talisman, sharing with it your desire for this ritual; and light your candles or incense, as you like.

Consider what issue you would like to receive a sign about right now. Maybe there is a recent ritual you created, and you want to know if it is going to be effective or not. Perhaps there is a health or relationship issue that you need insight on. Do you have concerns around your current job or creative endeavor? Are you wondering if a specific holy helper is right for you to work with?

Whatever it is, write down a bit about the situation in your Making Magic journal. Ask the question about this situation that you would most like to have answered. This is your call.

Breathe in a blessing on the call and exhale in gratitude.

Then think about what kind of a response you would like to receive. For instance, if you are asking a yes-or-no question, then what sign or omen might symbolize yes for you? It can be anything: the color orange, the smell of lemons, a bird feather, a specific song on the radio, the word *love*. Determine the same thing for the no answer.

If you are asking a more open-ended question, then what responses might be appropriate for its answer? Again, this can be anything.

My advice is to keep it open. Better to ask for a feather than a yellow feather. If you do ask for something specific, then be aware that it might show up in a unique way. Someone who asks to see oranges may instead see an orange flag as their response.

Note in your Making Magic journal what signs you are asking for.

Breathe in a blessing on yourself and exhale in gratitude.

Continue with your day and notice if you receive the response you were looking for. Give it at least three days. Make a note of your findings.

FIELD NOTES FROM THE EXTRAORDINARY

Opening to the possibility of learning that your holy helpers have been around you all along, allowing the sacred imagination to dream up what the perfect home for magic might look and feel like, creating an altar reflecting this home where everyday treasures are held with clearer eyes—in all of these cases we have opened ourselves up to the experience of call and response rooted in the extraordinary. In many ways, it is the most subjective and personal of relationships, but one that also leaves an impression. Whatever else we may know or not know, when it comes to our own unique holy helpers, the altar that is best suited for work that needs to be done, the talisman that is the perfect fit, the magic that will be absolutely effective, we will have gotten it just right because the time has been taken to heed and make the calls and to listen for the responses.

Synchronicity, a term coined by Carl Jung, speaks directly to this idea of call and response within the extraordinary.[2] It describes the occasion of asking for or receiving definite information found within liminal experience, and then discovering that this information has shown up in full and recognizable form in the everyday world. This phenomenon of synchronicity is one that all who remember their magic have in common, and it is potent enough that many a rational skeptic who would otherwise turn away or ignore the experience of the extraordinary completely do not, because they have seen in plain sight how the everyday and the extraordinary are constantly in communication with each other. Even Sigmund Freud, who, in *The Interpretation of Dreams*, denied the oracular powers of dreams, nevertheless admitted, perhaps begrudgingly, that dreams are not random nonsense and the ancients at least had one thing right: that dreams possess a *meaning* that cannot be denied.[3] Dreams offer ample material for self-work and the assessment of life choices and actions, but even more, they possess the capacity to open into the extraordinary. Some cultures, families, and individuals have never forgotten this fact.

For most of our history, dreams and divination have been concomitant phenomena. Dreams were considered to be oracular by the ancient world and our more recent ancestors, proceeding all the way up to and even through the Age of Enlightenment. In many cultures and families, dreams are still held in this way. They can be reminders of the past or portents of the future, and they have staying power, striking a chord, sounding the depths of the soul, and remaining easy to remember, even years after the fact. Such dreams are considered to be calls and responses made between us and the extraordinary.

For the ones who have not forgotten, these dreams are sometimes referred to as "true dreams," and the experience of dreaming this type of dream is known as "dreaming true." When we listen to dreams and take them seriously, we draw a distinction between true dreams and other kinds of dreaming, which might be more like a daily digest reflecting at random the day's or week's experiences or anxieties about tomorrow. True dreams tend to be rare. Because of their nature, it is doubtful whether we can contrive to make this sort of dreaming take place more frequently. Their material must be sorted and sifted with care; their messages are often like Russian doll sets, one nested inside of another, inside of another. For this reason, true dreams, even those that are fairly brief and simple, may stay with us for days, months, and even years after we initially dream them. True dreams may take many years to reveal their full implications for our lives.

Throughout life, you likely have had at least one dream that has stood out for you, shining or shadowy in its depth, troubling or comforting—or very often both. What I have found among my own clients and students is that the true dreams we have and carry with us are actually quite clear. The problem is, we don't always receive them with the same clarity with which they come to us. But we know in our hearts, if we can allow ourselves to listen, exactly what they mean and precisely what they ask of us. And after we allow ourselves to receive the dream with clarity, the trick is responding appropriately, taking the needed actions, making the necessary plan, committing to a particular course of action.

Before we can learn how to respond to dreams, we need to learn how to listen to dreams. We must learn what the dream wants—that is, why dreams are there in the first place. Moreover, we have to get a feel for the clarity that is native to them. *The clarity dreams want* is not so much the clarity of rational analysis but that of reflection and of love. A dream wants to be held, remembered, given a place; it wants to nourish you. A dream, thus, will be carried in the memory, even if you understood nothing about it. In most cases, all that is needed is for you to bear loving, marveling witness to the dream.

When we pay attention to our dreams and listen to the calls and responses they carry forward, we are performing an act of divination. Usually when we think of divination, what typically comes to mind are divination systems and devices like the tarot. This idea comes from misunderstanding the nature of divination. Divination is not a device. It is not found or bound into any one system. Rather, it is the act of paying attention to the ways and moments where the extraordinary and the everyday come together; it is another way of listening for and making calls, and of sending out and receiving responses.

The earliest diviners were viewed as having a special connection with the sacred that allowed them not only to see into the future but also, more importantly, to make essential connections that would help their communities flourish and thrive. Poets and singers in most traditions, including the ancient Greeks and Indians, were understood to hold a divinatory power. Musicians today hold the same power—even if unnamed—to mark out the essential connections that millions are drawn to.

Like magic, divination has been with humankind forever, and like magic, divination has run the course from being accepted, honored, and viewed as essential to being turned into something frightening and evil, driven completely underground, and finally to being labeled crazy, ignorant, and superstitious. The powers of divination are, in fact, exercised everywhere in mainstream life, but they are not recognized as such, and thus, as nameless, homeless wanderers, they inhabit Main Street and Wall Street. In other quarters, divination is experiencing a renaissance. Tarot coloring books, oracle decks for children, and systems like the tarot or Lenormand cards are enjoying wide reception, signaling that more people than ever before are interested in divination and the many ways it can be applied to human life in the modern world.

Just as call and response is an experience everyone engages with every single day, so are dreams and divination. When it comes to both, there is much less to learn than we might anticipate, because we already engage in both actions on a daily basis. All of us already have the experience needed to begin cultivating the sources of meaningful divination and getting underway with it, prior to ever picking up a divinatory device or tool.

In performing the rituals in this book, you have already engaged in divination multiple times. Working with talismans, discovering and engaging with holy helpers, feeling your way into making the altar *just so*, and getting to know the magical goods with which you had unknowingly stocked your kitchen are a few examples of incipient divination in action. Long before you picked up this book, though, you divined. Divination is so natural to us that the discovery of it is something like a discovery that we have been breathing this whole time without any effort.

As we have seen, paying attention to dreams, bearing loving witness to them, listening to their call and response, is itself an act of divination. Divination is not applied to dreams, but we bear within ourselves, in our dreaming every night, ample divinatory material to work with, for a dream is the soul's entrance into the art of divination. The attempt to understand a true dream we are gifted with is simply an act of bringing to fruition a natural or spontaneous process that had already started when we were fast asleep and dreaming.

If we want to hone our native ability to divine, there are other aspects of our everyday experience that we can work with besides dreams. Divination begins with apparently inane activities, like guessing where the plot line in a movie or story might go next, to sincerer attempts at understanding how another person is feeling, or seeking out insight in order to make sense of how a given situation might unfold. When we pay attention to the meaning behind something, the subtext, the inner ideas, or when we consider the causes and the consequences of an action or a viewpoint or a belief, we are divining—no cards required.

You do not need to enroll in a class to hone your native capacity for divination. Let your own experience be your guide. Dedicate a notebook or a section of your Making Magic journal to daily divination. Go through your day, and when something captures your attention, make a note of it. It can be an image, a song, a weird coincidence, words, books, objects that show up and resonate with you, numbers that seem significant, a certain scent, or just a feeling that you have when you rounded that particular corner on the street.

Write down the moments that stand out. Sometimes there will be only one, sometimes there will be many, and on other days just a few. As always, there is no right or wrong with this; we are just playing and trying things out.

Once you have your list, go over it. Look at what you have noted and then ask yourself what information and insight the event(s) you wrote down give you about the day, the week, maybe even the month. In doing this, you are creating your own divination journal, and it will be relevant for your dream life as well because many of the same themes, objects, situations, and experiences will show up, often in different or modified forms, in your dream life.

RITUAL SLEEPING, WAKING, WALKING

If you wish to take your dreaming and divining further and want to combine the two, this is a ritual that will teach you how to do so. This ritual is meant to begin right before you go to bed and then continue into the next day.

TIME   1 night and day

MATERIALS
~ your Making Magic journal
~ a place to go for a fifteen- to twenty-minute walk at whatever pace works best

PROCESS

Perform the "Easy Breath Relax and Release" from chapter 2.

If there is a question or a situation in your life—big or small—that you are concerned about or need an answer on, write it down in your Making Magic journal.

Then, in writing, speech, or silence, ask that you receive a dream that will give you clarity on your question or situation.

Breathe in a blessing on yourself, exhaling in gratitude.

Go to bed as you normally would.

Upon waking, before doing anything else, write down anything about your dream(s) that you can recall. If you cannot recall anything, write down, "nothing."

Then go on with your day. When you are ready and have the opportunity, go for a fifteen- to twenty-minute walk at whatever pace is good for you.

Before you begin your walk, ask in writing, speech, or silence to receive a token that speaks to both your dreams (even if you cannot remember them) and the question or situation you are working on.

Go for your walk and pay attention to what you encounter during it.

Upon returning home, note what your experience of the walk was like. Consider how that experience and any encounters you may have had during it speak or do not speak to your dreams the night before and to your current question or situation.

If at any point you are feeling overwhelmed by information, ask, What can be put to good use right here and right now?

Pick one element from your dreams or walk and decide how it might practically apply to your life here and now. You do not have to apply the element at this point; just notice how you would or could apply it.

STEPPING STONES

- Write a quick note to one of your holy helpers. Think of it as a call. What kind of a response does it receive?

- Play with different kinds of divination. Hold a question in your mind and then flip open a book at random, placing your finger on a particular part of the page. (This is called *bibliomancy*.) Or hold a question in your mind and flip through radio stations or playlists until you feel compelled to stop. What does the current song tell you about your question?

- Share a striking dream with a friend and ask them to share one of theirs with you. Notice how taking your dream material more seriously makes you feel.

At this point in the journey, you may have begun to notice certain patterns and trends repeating. The starting point is straightforward, simple, and grounded in everyday life and experience. And from each starting point, you discover resources that are woven through and through with the extraordinary. Remembering magic and weaving the worlds back together is an act of bringing the soul back together wholly and completely. But it is also, and at the same time, an act of radicalism, of resistance. Dare to go to the roots, dare to know, in the fullest and deepest ways imaginable, what is really required for the mending and healing of the broken places. Never give in. This is the true power of call and response: we send out the calls that come straight from the heart, we receive the gift, and the overflow returns to strengthen us from the bones up.

Remembered magic cannot be bottled or systematized, only practiced again and again. And one of the primary places to practice it is in the act of praying down hard.

10

PRAYING DOWN HARD

[G]ive thanks for all your blessins'
Get on your knees and pray.
HANK WILLIAMS, "Thank God"[1]

In story and song, myth and legend, the wild places are the places of last resort. Heroes, prophetesses, soldiers, merchants, villains, saviors, and ordinary folk go into the wild places in the world in order to get stripped down to their bare bones. For it is in these uncharted and unmapped territories that the essential questions are best comprehended and explored: What do we actually require for survival? What do we care most about at the end of the day? What keeps us going? Why?

Stepping into this uncharted territory, we lose whatever is not essential, and in turn, we find ourselves distilled, refined, and honed. In wild places, there is less room for mistakes and more riding on every action. And it is for these reasons that throughout history, the wild places within ourselves and our world have been the best places to go and learn how to "pray down hard," to develop the bold heart to ask for what is really desired or what is truly needed. It is here that we learn to ask for what we really want, discover why we really want it, and give our request physical breadth, depth, and shape in the form of a petition.

In the story of Golden Locks, the ask is simple: Will the Bear People teach the intrepid youngster? Will they spend some time with her, explaining what is possible when it comes to making magic? She does not receive an answer right away but rather has to wait for it patiently, demonstrating that she is really committed to the task she has set before herself.

Typically, the requests are straightforward in the stories. Cinderella wants to go to the ball. Hansel and Gretel want to find their way back home. The miller's daughter wants to learn the trick of spinning straw into gold. Basic requests, upfront asks, catalyze an entire sequence of events, giving us a story and heroes and heroines who are utterly transformed within and without.

It may seem strange to see a chapter about prayer in a book about magic. Even stranger will be the idea that prayer is not only magical but also a deeply erotic act. If you have ever seen someone praying from the deepest places of their heart and with an extraordinary single-mindedness, you will catch the scent of the wild we are calling magic.

Prayer and petition-making are two sacred arts employed in magic the world over, and they are rooted in the most everyday experiences: wanting, desiring, yearning, hoping, needing, and dreaming. This is the Eros, the desire. The acts called *prayer* are, in fact, so closely woven into magic that if you cannot pray, you cannot remember yourself back to your magic. Praying itself is an act done with the intention to enter into relation-ship with the extraordinary—even to call it down to the earth, so to speak, the way a lightning rod channels the electrical charge of the atmosphere, completes the circuit, and calls down lightning.

In this chapter, we are going to spend time in the part of our soul soil that has been marked up by Eros, desire. Along the way, we shall discover the prayers and petitions that are rooted precisely in those wants and desires. As Thomas Merton observed, one of the great problems in life is being far too satisfied with "an insufficient answer to a question we are afraid to ask."[2] Perhaps, if we are lucky, we might discover the courage that allows us to ask the most needed questions in our lives.

FIELD NOTES FROM THE EVERYDAY

What happens when you ask for what you want, what you desire, what you need? What have your experiences been? What has to happen before you even ask? Do you take time to get clear on what your wants and desires really are, or are they readily apparent? Do you stoke up your courage, do some breathing exercises, meditate before making the request? Do you wait until you are so strained that you have no other recourse than to ask for help, or do you ask quickly and loudly whenever you have need? When do you ask? How do you ask? Who do you ask? Are you more comfortable asking strangers or friends or family members? What inherited ideas do you bring to the table when it comes to asking? What needs to happen in your life practically, emotionally, and intellectually before you are ready to ask for what you want, need, desire?

Asking is an action in its own right. Asking for what we really want seems as though it might be the easiest thing in the world to do, and yet it may be one of the most difficult and therefore most urgent of all of our actions. In this conflict is the substance of many a fairy tale: Be careful, they tell us, with what you wish for. Yet at the same time, you must make a wish.

Why is asking so difficult? Asking for something from a place of genuine desire exposes us, rendering us vulnerable. This vulnerability can be experienced as intimately as a threat to life and limb. Even more, genuine asking involves a tacit commitment to that request. It is not enough simply to ask, especially if it is regarding some genuine want or need; we have to make a commitment to the thing we're seeking. More essentially, we must be prepared to commit to whatever practical actions will support the desired goal. We may want what we want, but we may not be prepared to do whatever it takes to get it. It is exactly here, in the tension exposed by our true desire and the means to achieve it, that something fruitful appears.

No sooner is the territory of word and deed traversed than fresh difficulties arise. First of all, desire is tricky: it is not always immediately obvious what we really need or desire. A thousand desires compete for our attention and recognition.

The second challenge is that even when we do develop a clear idea of the object of desire, it can be difficult to put into words. Discovering what we really yearn for brings us face to face with the ineffable, that which cannot be spoken or put into words. Many of our most urgent matters encounter tremendous difficulties when we try to explain and express even relatively simple concepts with words. How much more difficult is it for us to utter our highest dreams and desires—at an altar, to holy helpers, in rituals—when we experience difficulties speaking them even over our own hearts?

Given this situation, it may seem that there is no point in even making the attempt to put such difficult things into words. But, in fact, there is the greatest need to. Why? Because there is no other way to get the clearest and deepest possible sense of what the ineffable is like—in living color and movement. Intimate knowledge of that which goes beyond words is found only by pressing to the limits what can be put into words—by really exploring words and how they relate to the reality people live with every day. Words are not perfect, but we ought to trust the sense they point to.

RITUAL GETTING RIGHT WITH WANTING

A lot of sage advice centers around the idea of becoming unattached—to outcomes, desires, hopes, dreams, and situations we have no control over. And while I do not dispute that un-attachment can and does support us in certain ways, I have also seen from the most ancient and varied sources—from the Mahabharata, to the works of Plato, to the Bible, to the Buddhist sutras—that we are not and cannot be bigger than our desires. The only way to come into right relationship with yearning, desire, and wanting is to first acknowledge what it is that we yearn for, desire, and want. And believe it or not, this is usually the hardest step.

TIME   20 to 30 minutes

MATERIALS
- ~ your Making Magic journal
- ~ a door (optional)
- ~ a special talisman (optional)
- ~ candles (optional)
- ~ incense (optional)

PROCESS

Perform the "Easy Breath Relax and Release" from chapter 2. Open your door; touch your talisman, sharing with it your desire for this ritual; and light your candles or incense, as you like.

What do you want? Right here and right now? What do you desire? What do you yearn for? Write the answers down in your Making Magic journal.

Breathe in a blessing on those answers, exhaling in gratitude.

Now consider, what do you need? Write the answers down in your Making Magic journal.

Breathe in a blessing on those answers and notice whether they are the same as or different from what you want.

What would a ritual that honored these wants and needs look like? What would it sound like, taste like, smell like, and feel like?

Create that ritual. Write it down, paint it, sing it, act it out.

Afterward, note in your Making Magic journal how you feel.

Breathe in a final blessing on yourself. Exhale in gratitude.

FIELD NOTES FROM THE EXTRAORDINARY

The magical potential of prayer and petition-making shows up in the everyday relationship between word and deed. We need not think of ourselves as particularly spiritual or holy or prayerful in order to pray. Prayer is something we all have in common, whether we realize it or not. For prayer, at its most basic root, is the act of asking for something, and we have all done that. If you know how to ask for something, then you know how to pray. In truth, so many of the acts we engage in on a daily basis are acts of prayer. Wherever there is an ask, there we find a prayer.

As Rumi says, "There are hundreds of ways to kneel and kiss the ground."[3] Wherever there is a need, there we will find our best way of praying down hard. Just as the ways of asking are blessedly diverse, so are the ways of prayer.

We can hip sway, flamenco step, or split leap our way into our prayers. Prayers are carried on drum and rattle, clap and finger snap, and arched eyebrow. Painting, drawing, writing out, writing down, and creation in all forms are prayers. Prayers can be verbalized with sound and rhythm. They can be given physicality through motion and form, and they can be created through silent contemplation, concentration, and reverence. Building your altar is a form of prayer. Finding and opening your doors, reaching out to touch the extraordinary, communing with your holy helpers—all prayer, all potent.

Petition is actually just another word for prayer, and petition-making is another way to describe the act of praying. However, within magical traditions, the term *petition* often indicates a prayer that has been inscribed in some manner—on paper, a piece of wax, a metal tablet, into soft clay or wet sand, into a piece of bread before it is baked, in the air with smoke or your finger or a sharp knife. A petition is a way of physically representing prayers and the deepest asks. Petitions are created with words, with entire sentences or paragraphs. Every book I have ever read is a long petition. This one asks you to remember, seek out, and start making magic at any point on your journey. For those who keep a journal, the journal is—guess what?—a petition. Petitions can also be formed of symbols, visual art, and simple glyphs. As soon as a prayer has been given physical form, a petition is created.

The formation of petitions is much more common than we might think. Flags, be they for state or country or prayer, are petitions. Vision boards, tiny glass bottles filled with insect wings, beads, and bits of paper carrying the needed words—all petitions. Pot metal *milagros* tied to vibrantly colored ribbons, tattoos inscribed on skin, your very own name—each one is an example of a petition. We are surrounded by them. In fact, petitions and the prayers they carry are so ubiquitous that in many magical practices, the creation of a petition is itself the whole of a ritual: You ask for what you need to ask for. You commit to the actions that will be required to achieve your goal. You create a physical reminder of your ability to pray down hard and of your agreement to allow that prayer to exercise its full work—changing you, altering your experience and your life, from the inside out. Nothing more needs to be done or said.

Prayer. Petition. Asking for what the heart desires. Committing. Many stories tangle around the notions of what is and is not allowed, what can and cannot be rightfully or lawfully pursued, what counts or doesn't as a prayer straight from the heart. So many broken places can be stirred up by this process that they threaten to overwhelm before we find the blessing ways. But as lovers of the wild animal we call magic, we may take heart. We start with where we are, here and now.

What does prayer mean to you? What does it look like? What could it look like? What kind of prayer would feel nourishing, sustaining, and useful? What prayers feel the opposite? What rules and mind-sets around prayers have you bought into, and what would happen if you allowed yourself to consider alternative possibilities? How would you pray? Who or what would you pray to? What would you pray for? And how would you make those prayers physical? Are you a lover of sand and salt and water? Then perhaps your petitions will be made mostly from those materials. Are you a baker who delights in the idea of creating intricate symbols for blessing on top of every cake and muffin? There is the way you make petitions. Gardeners will find their best words inscribed through dirt and seed and green-growing things. Lovers will inscribe their petitions on the insides of each other's mouths with swirling, saliva-slicked tongues.

There are wrong ways to pray and create petitions—any way that is not your own, that was forced onto you or accepted by you without due thought and reflection. Perhaps it will turn out, upon deep consideration, that these ways were right after all. But rightness enters into the picture only because you decided it was so. There are right ways to pray and make petitions—hundreds, thousands, and millions of them, as many ways as there are people and creatures on the land.

Remembered magic is deep magic, the earliest and first wild magic, which is much more about learning, listening, and standing in wonder of what is possible, as opposed to inflicting or enforcing our limited viewpoint onto the whole of the cosmos. As such, magic is always at least as much directed toward inner understanding and transformation as it is to external change.

As we call back magic, we remember, honor, acknowledge, and care for the many desires that move through us every day, as well as the problems of coming to know them well and deeply. This is the foundation of prayer and petition-making within the sacred arts. We reflect upon our actual needs and desires, and then we ask for and seek out an answer. We resolve to show up and, with a ready heart, stay open to the answer, in whatever form it may happen to take. This is why prayer and petition-making are always found in rituals, because it is important to know why we are creating a specific rite, and "the ask" behind the ritual is what provides this information, provides the required sense of direction and purpose, as we venture into time beyond time to make magic.

Sending out prayers and making petitions are the everyday acts that also happen to be the vehicles for these asks within the extraordinary. Like in the story of Golden Locks, sometimes the request will not be granted immediately—or at all. It is for this reason that prayer, petition-making, and faith are often aligned with each other. Because it does require faith and courage and devotion to ask for what you want and need, all the while taking seriously the possibility that you may not get it or the even more frightening alternative—that you actually will.

RITUAL BODY BLESSING

Just as our bodies are our first altars, they are also origin points for our wants, needs, and desires. This is a ritual prayer and petition-making that honors this most precious origin point.

TIME 15 to 20 minutes

MATERIALS
- ~ your Making Magic journal
- ~ a full-length mirror
- ~ plain olive or almond oil or a ritual anointing oil of your choice
- ~ a door (optional)
- ~ a special talisman (optional)
- ~ candles (optional)
- ~ incense (optional)

PROCESS
Perform the "Easy Breath Relax and Release" from chapter 2. Open your door; touch your talisman, sharing with it your desire for this ritual; and light your candles or incense, as you like.

Look at yourself in the full-length mirror. (You may be clothed or naked, as you like.)

Look down at your feet. Breathe in a blessing on your feet and exhale in gratitude.

Then consider: What do you want for your feet? What do you need for them? Where do you want your feet to take you?

Then say aloud or write down in your journal, "Blessed be my feet, for they . . ." filling in the blank with the want, need, or desire. Write it down and then say it aloud. Once you have done so, dip your finger into the oil and make a shape or symbol that is meaningful to you on both of your feet. It can be a star, heart, cross, spiral—you get to choose what resonates for you.

Repeat this process for your legs, knees, thighs, sex, belly, chest/breasts, hands, arms, shoulders, neck, lips, eyes, and head, and for any other parts of your body you want to include. As you create a prayer for each part of your body, turn it into a petition by inscribing a particular shape (they can all be the same or not) on that part of your body too.

Once you have completed the process, go through your Making Magic journal and read the prayer in its entirety aloud over yourself.

Final act: Pick one thing that you are focused on right now in your life. Create a prayer for it and then turn that prayer into a petition.

STEPPING STONES

- Make a compendium of symbols and glyphs that speak to you. Some common choices are stars, moons, crosses, and spirals. Take a glass of water, hold a concern in your mind, inscribe one of your symbols over the water, and then drink it. How do you feel?

- Light a stick of incense in the morning as you are getting ready for your day. Take the stick and write in the air a word that has meaning to you. It can be a single word or a positive affirmation. Notice how you feel after the fact.

- Jot down a few notes about a situation concerning you. Take the paper you have written the notes down on, turn it 90 degrees toward yourself, and then inscribe your name across the notes enough times so that it completely covers them. This is an act of asserting your sovereignty over the situation. How does it feel?

Another side of prayer and petition-making is the act of saying *thank you*. It is easy to forget about this. When we pray down hard, when we make our petitions, something deep within our soul is exposed. This is vulnerable work. It transforms us, as magic is wont to do, from the inside out. And so it is appropriate to thank the materials we work with and the holy helpers we call upon, and to thank ourselves for standing in witness to ourselves, as we press forward with this magical and holy work.

Just as there are as many ways to pray and petition as there are people in the world, there are an equal number of ways to say thank you. So find yours, and at the same time, make every *thank you* that you utter in your everyday experience a little blessing upon the person that you thank. This is one more way to make magic, one more way to weave in all that is extraordinary into the everyday.

II

WATERS AND WASHING

L'acqua é il vetturale della natura.
Water is the vital force of nature.
LEONARDO DA VINCI[1]

Human life is surrounded by water—indeed, comprised of it. As Leonardo da Vinci, a passionate and lifelong student of the mysterious substance, observed, water possesses a power of movement that is impossible to pin down. No matter where human dwelling places are found—on high mountain, in hot desert, on great plain, in fecund wetland, or on craggy coastline—humankind's relationship with water shapes it as surely as the Colorado River shaped the ridge lines of the Grand Canyon, day after day, moment after moment. The relationship we have with water begins long before we draw our first breath of air; it begins when we are dancing, floating, and fluttering in the ocean of our mothers' wombs. That ocean is internalized into human substance, growing into bodies that are composed primarily of this same element, water. Our connection to water is both physical and philosophical at the same time. The Chinese Daoists, led by the teachings of their sage Laozi, claimed that water was the strongest of all of the elements—stronger than wood or stone or metal—because it had the power to wear away rock and the range to move from the highest to the lowest places. Access to clean water is sometimes a source of both privilege and guilt, a tangible reminder of how blessed we are in the developed world to have it and how much of a struggle it is for large swaths of the planet to find similar access.

As we travel through the everyday terrains of soul and story and reflect on our vast experiences, certain topographic features arise again and again in our soul soil. We find that within us there are deep wells, strong-running springs, vast oceans, and swift-moving rivers. Our experience of these waters roots us in the arts of spiritual cleansing and sacred bathing—activities that we have performed on a daily basis for most of our lives without knowing their inner magic.

The story of Golden Locks reminds us of the power of water, for the caves of the Bear People are bounded by a rushing river that the tired heroine must find a way to cross. This is a feature we find in many fairy tales, myths, and legends, from the story of the isle of Avalon, where the dying King Arthur was taken to be healed and honored, to that of the three rivers that feed the roots of the Nordic Tree of Life, Yggdrasil. The extraordinary and the ordinary often share an aquatic boundary with each other. Water itself is a deeply liminal element, capable of taking on whatever shape and whatever form of whatever vessel it might be poured into, and able to appear seemingly out of nowhere, seeping up and through dry ground and covering the world with great rains. But it is the cleansing element of water, the fact that it washes away all detritus so that all that remains is what is most essential and needed, that makes it such a perfect boundary marker. Here we are taught another lesson by magic: to let our inner rivers and waters flow forth, for this is what calls up life.

FIELD NOTES FROM THE EVERYDAY

Like all that is wild, like nature itself, water is easy to take for granted because it plays such a pervasive role in our lives and takes so many different forms. It is ever present, and the familiarity we human beings have with it has a way of blinding our mind's eye to its presence and magic. So how can we begin to let those scales drop away from our eyes and see this element and its gifts clearly? As always, the starting point is with what we know best: the experiences we have actually had with water.

Get practical. Reflect upon the relationship that you have on a daily basis with water. How much of it do you drink? What is your favorite way of working with it? Do you love a long bath illuminated by candlelight to round out your day, or do you prefer a brisk shower? Is watering your garden in the early morning or evening hours the most satisfying activity for you? Does the promise of a boiling pot of water on the stovetop make your eyes bright with anticipation?

Begin with the experiences that are closest to you, including your memories. Do you have any that feature water in a prominent manner? If so, recognize these memories as the teachers they are and spend some time with them. Then, think bigger. What are the naturally occurring bodies of water closest to you? Who loved, honored, utilized, and protected them in times past? What plants, animals, and people depend on them today? What is their current state? Learn where your drinking water comes from and what has to happen before it makes it into your tap.

Water heals, as it is used to make medicines and then called upon again to clean and purify the hurt places before those medicines are applied. Water nourishes—from the water (and all libations) that we drink, to the water that is used in growing our food, to the water we use to wash our food before eating it. Water inspires stories—of floods and monsters of the deep; sunken treasures and arks of animals; and one of my favorites, given to my husband by a devout Catholic nun, of the rain that falls in our desert climate being God's pearlescent semen impregnating the earth with good, green life. Water saves—from the theological perspective, it saves through sacred baths and baptisms found in religious and spiritual traditions across time and culture, and from the practical perspective, it saves because without water there is simply no life.

The act of bathing speaks directly to water's ability to clean, cleanse, and wash away all that needs to be removed. It includes our daily acts of bathing, showering, and cleaning our homes and vehicles. When I tell my students that one of the most magical things they can do is take a bath, I rarely have to say anything more, for we intuitively know that the time we take to shower and bathe is time touched by wild magic, and the space in which we do so is space imbued with the scent of the sacred.

Consider your own bathing rituals right here and right now. Begin with the fundamental question, What needs to be washed away, removed, released? And then, What kind of bathing appeals to you the most? A brisk shower or a slow bath? If you use products like bubbles, soap, bath salts, or body scrubs, what products do you use, and why did you select them? Do you love to bathe in the privacy of your own home, or do you feel most connected to your remembered magic when you immerse yourself into a wildly running river, the cresting waves of a great ocean, or the green depths of a limestone spring? What elements need to be in place to change your bathing experience from one that is merely practical and about physically cleaning yourself to one that is also extraordinary and capable of washing away deeper marks and struggles?

What features need to be present to make your bathing experiences truly magical? Do you need candles, living plants, special music, or a certain set of clothes to change into after your bathing rite is completed? After your bathing experience, do you need to anoint yourself with a scented oil or a lotion, bless your body, spend extra time washing your hair, be wrapped up in the softest blanket, or allow yourself to air-dry naked? Do you feel the need to take some of the bath or shower water used in ritual and dispose of it in a specific way—at a crossroads as the sun sets or rises, at the base of a healthy tree, as a way to water your garden? Do you need to watch the last drops of water swirl down the drain, knowing that as they do so, they are carrying whatever you released on their currents?

Sacred bathing belongs to the more general category of spiritual cleaning. Most of us clean and straighten up our homes, our vehicles, and our work spaces on a regular basis. Even those of us who have domestic help still find ourselves cleaning—from washing up a few dirty dishes in the sink to mopping the entire house. Cleaning is an ever-present practice that yields yet another opportunity for the everyday and the extraordinary to touch. When we clean, we are asking both practically and magically, What needs to be cleaned up, cleaned out, and put back into order?

Once you have become clear about what your space (remembering that "space" here includes your living space and your vehicles, as well as your work spaces) requires in the way of cleaning, then consider how you like to clean. What products do you use? What botanicals and minerals keep showing up as you go through these processes? What different kinds of people and holy helpers want to assist you in your work?

As you did with bathing, think about what needs to happen to make the cleaning experience more attuned to the extraordinary. Are there specific times of day when you like to clean? Does cleaning give you an opportunity to get the entire family involved in a ritual? Does cleaning feel more magical when you begin by blessing your space or yourself in some manner or by making an offering at your altar? Is there a specific outfit you like to wear when you clean, music that you like to listen to, or a libation that you like to have on hand as you go about your work? Once you have finished cleaning a space, is there a way that you feel called to mark it as having been restored to order and touched by the extraordinary? Do you want to light a candle for blessing each room? Go through your entire home, censing it with fragrant smoke? Place a medallion or charm for protection in your vehicle? Create a petition for your workplace desk that is then secreted away behind the picture of your family or favorite pet? After cleansing your spaces, do you need then to wash yourself and engage in some sacred bathing? Do you simply want to rest and dive into a good book, appreciating the work you have done?

There is also an internal act of cleansing, which is most effectively accomplished by doing nothing more and nothing less than drinking water. Just as our mental, emotional, and spiritual needs will shift and be reprioritized as we remember our magic, our physical needs will also undergo a transformation.

As sacred artists remembering our magic, we often find we need more time to sleep, desire to get up earlier or stay up later, want certain foods more than others (even if we were not very food aware before), and need to drink more water than we have in the past. This last need is generated in part by the fact that as we live, work, and walk in both worlds, we become more permeable, able to take in more information and more experiences, finding that our levels of empathy and feeling intensify. Greater sensitivity to pleasure brings heightened sensitivity to pain. The need for moderation arises from this tension, and keeping the physical streams of the body running smoothly and cleanly as much as possible is one of the best ways to exert that moderation. Water nourishes, restores, and allows for flushing out the internal impurities that are not of use, so that greater space and capacity are created to focus on what is.

RITUAL LET THE RIVERS RUN

The next time you drink water, allow yourself to open up to this most everyday act. This ritual supports you in doing exactly that.

TIME 10 minutes

MATERIALS

- ~ your Making Magic journal
- ~ a glass of water that you can drink
- ~ a door (optional)
- ~ a special talisman (optional)
- ~ candles (optional)
- ~ incense (optional)

PROCESS

Perform the "Easy Breath Relax and Release" from chapter 2. Open your door; touch your talisman, sharing with it your desire for this ritual; and light your candles or incense, as you like.

Take some time to consider the following questions: Where do you feel parched at the moment? Where are you in need of restoration and soothing? What have you taken inside of yourself—from food, to problems that are not your own, to another person's bad attitude—that needs to be flushed out now? Where could you benefit from a little more moisture, depth, and lucidity?

Write down your responses to the questions in your Making Magic journal.

Once you have written down your responses, take a deep breath, and as you exhale, blow your breath over the cup of water, blessing it.

Drink the water. Allow yourself to feel the water move from your mouth, teeth, and tongue all the way down and through your body, running through you like a river, picking up any internal debris along the way that needs to be flushed out.

Say thank you to the water and the magical work it is doing even now within you.

Go on with the rest of your day.

Final act: After you perform this ritual, the next time you have to go to the bathroom to urinate will be the final act of releasing. Once you have finished your business, bless yourself in whatever way makes sense, filling the internal spaces left behind in your body with blessing.

FIELD NOTES FROM THE EXTRAORDINARY

The power of water on earth is incomprehensibly great, beyond the reach of our capacity to master it, and our use of it is miniscule in comparison with its grandeur. Even the largest hydroelectric or river-diverting engineering pales in comparison with the dynamo of global ocean currents that drive weather patterns.

While the cleansing qualities of a temperate use of gently flowing waters have been the object of much-needed attention, we should never stop reflecting on the storms and the power of storms. We would do well to keep track of the experience of storms that we pass through. What is our experience before a storm arrives? How do we respond during the storm? After the storm has passed, what changes have been made to the area affected?

Just as the land where we live contains water, our soul soil also holds swift rivers, vast oceans, and deep springs. These interior waters are the places understood to hold the human capacity for deep feeling and emotion, creativity, love and compassion, vitality and nourishment. And just like bodies of water in the surrounding world, our interior waters can be dammed up, walled off, covered over, and blocked in a variety of ways. These waters can also be polluted. Sometimes this is done by others or is a result of the toxic aspects of the culture at large, and sometimes we do it to ourselves without realizing it. Having set up house in multiple arid lands, I can tell you from firsthand experience that the presence or the absence of water in our surrounding world presses us to ask hard questions about our internal waters. Consider where does your life feel dry, uninspired, lacking creativity, fecundity, and fertility? Where are there places that have become too tough and hard and not nearly tender enough? Where has your soul soil been in drought for year upon year, so that all you can find there is dry dust and cracks in the ground? Where is the spark of life lacking or completely absent?

After considering what makes you feel dried up and devitalized, consider the opposite. What calls up your life and creativity? What makes you feel like your inner landscape is well irrigated and flowing with wide rivers or caressed by ocean waves? What are the ways that you best clean up the hurt places in your life? What are the medicines that help you heal most readily and completely?

Our work here calls us to an awareness of the places that feel broken, the parts of life and the stories, beliefs, and habits that devitalize us from the inside out. Working with water in an intentional manner can also highlight these places, for we become acutely aware of where precisely there is lack. It is natural to feel that there is not enough water in the whole world to slake the deepest soul thirst and soothe the most parched places of our hearts. It is true: there is not enough water in the world to quench that thirst. But there is enough water in each of us. When you live in a desert, as I have for most of my life, you come to know this as fact. There is good water, strong and flowing, usually many miles beneath the surface, and when the thunderclouds come in and the wind begins to blow just so, the sheer rocks themselves begin to usher forth rivers and streams, and the well that springs up from the deepest self carries on its waves life-bestowing and life-affirming blessings.

RITUAL BASIC SACRED BATH

This is a very basic ritual for sacred bathing. It can be adopted and adapted in a variety of ways and should be taken in the spirit it is given: as a loose framework. If you do not have access to a bathtub, then you can take the suggested herbs, bundle them into a muslin cloth, hang the bundle on your shower nozzle, and take a sacred shower instead.

TIME   30 to 60 minutes

MATERIALS
- ~ a bathtub
- ~ your Making Magic journal
- ~ 1 cup Epsom salt
- ~ 3 bay leaves
- ~ ½ cup dried peppermint (you can also use peppermint tea bags)
- ~ ½ cup dried lavender
- ~ 3 drops lemongrass essential oil or 1 sliced stalk of lemongrass if you can find it fresh
- ~ clean towels (optional)
- ~ lotion or anointing oil of your choice
- ~ clean clothes
- ~ a door (optional)
- ~ a special talisman (optional)
- ~ candles (optional)
- ~ incense (optional)

PROCESS

Perform the "Easy Breath Relax and Release" from chapter 2. Open your door; touch your talisman, sharing with it your desire for this ritual; and light your candles or incense, as you like.

Affirm and acknowledge that you are going to take a sacred bath. Take some time to consider what needs to be washed away and removed by this bath.

If you have written a petition for this bath, say it aloud as you begin to run the water.

Add the ingredients to the water, beginning with the Epsom salt and ending with the lemongrass essential oil or stalk of fresh lemongrass.

Bathe in whatever ways are best for you.

When you are ready, emerge from the bath and allow yourself to air-dry or dry off with clean towels.

Anoint yourself with the oil or lotion you selected.

Put on clean clothes.

Take a few moments to reflect on your experience of this sacred bath in your Making Magic journal.

Breathe in a blessing on your body. Exhale in gratitude.

STEPPING STONES

- Create a sacred spray. Get a spray bottle, fill it with water, add a few drops of your favorite essential oils, and use this quick version of sacred water to spritz yourself and your home, as you like.

- Make moon water. Fill up a clear glass jar with water and leave the top of it open. Set it outside under a full moon. Drink it down the next morning and note the texture, taste, and feel of the water as you do. Notice too how your body feels after drinking it.

- Don't have time for a full sacred bath? Give yourself a footbath instead. Fill a basin with warm water, and add a teaspoon of baking soda, some lemon and lime slices, and any essential oils you like. After soaking your feet, pick out an oil or lotion to anoint your feet. Cleansing and anointing the feet is an ancient practice that honors one of the most sensitive (and taken for granted) parts of our bodies.

The cleansing and purification of physical spaces is of great concern in many magical traditions because the relationship between us and the physical spaces we occupy is so foundational. Our lives are surrounded at all times with their own particular horizon. As we recollect our magic and new elements are drawn into it, the physical spaces within which we spend most of our time will also take on greater importance. Those spaces, like the place of the body, are like apertures into eternity.

Even if cleaning has not been your favorite activity up until this point, it may soon be, for it turns out that cleansing can proffer great pleasure and peace. You should at least expect the act of cleansing to occupy a greater, more central place as you proceed further along your path. As you explore the world of washing and bathing, you will do well to remember that the act of ritual bathing is not limited to a full bathing experience. Washing the hands or the feet, the face or hair, are also forms of sacred bathing, deeply rooted in long-standing tradition and the extraordinary.

An effect of working closely with the extraordinary is that the old orders by which life is organized—from the sense of time and scheduling, to the sense of priority and meaning—begin to shift ground. Remember that *extraordinary* means literally "out of the regular order of things" and that trafficking with the extraordinary also inspires us to find new organizing principles or to reorder life in fresh ways, especially in ways that are unique, custom-made, and more authentic to who we actually are, while honoring what we actually want. The place where this reordering actually happens is, more times than not, in our everyday actions, like bathing or drinking water. It can even begin with that first sip of your morning libation.

12

HOLDING SPACE

It's the hollow that makes the pot work . . .

LAOZI, *Taoteching* (Red Pine, translator)[1]

After working with water, which takes the shape of any vessel, we now turn our attention to the vessels themselves, for these everyday items are also filled with the extraordinary. In the tale of "Golden Locks and the Three Bears," the container that holds the action and the substance of the story is the cave. It creates a solid boundary and protected space in which Golden Locks can take her time, engaging with the Bear People and the tasks they set before her. The magic made is contained by the cave's stony walls. Here, magic is protected, concentrated, and allowed to unfold in its own way and its own time, with no outside interruption. This is one of the primary gifts of containers: they hold space—particular, finite space—and they are able to hold whatever needs to be held so that it may be allowed to ripen and fully come into its own. It is here that we can learn how to hold magic and learn how to be held by it in turn.

If you have ever encountered a wild animal for any significant amount of time, you know a special kind of space-holding is required for the encounter. It goes something like this: you sit or you stand very still and very quiet, and you wait—but you wait in such a way that every nerve and fiber of your body is alive, aware, and at attention. You are waiting for that moment of eye contact, the slow approach, the possibility that perhaps, just perhaps, there is some common ground that you and this magical creature share. In holding the space this way, you have, for a moment, become a vessel for holding magic.

Throughout this chapter, we are going to investigate that magical family of the most common, everyday items: containers. From mismatched Tupperware to imported glass bowls, and covering every jar, bottle, vase, and box in between, we will cross over the valleys, ravines, and calderas where magic has been made and held forever, and we will see how these most ordinary of objects point to the magical art of holding space. We will begin with our everyday experience of containers and then move into the various kinds of magic we can make with them, as everyday and extraordinary meet up once more.

FIELD NOTES FROM THE EVERYDAY

One of the three things anyone needs in order to have a fighting chance in a wilderness survival situation is a container of some kind. The other two, a sharp knife and some form of cordage like rope or twine, make immediate sense. But the notion that containers—cups, bowls, jars, and vessels of all kinds—are equally essential is easy to overlook. When we think about it, we immediately see how essential various containers are for both the ordinary and the extreme situations of life. Beginning with the very first few hours of each day—with the cups that hold our coffee and tea, the drawers that hold our underthings, the bowls and plates that we use to prepare our breakfasts, and even the digital containers that store files for us—we would not be able to function without various kinds of containers, ways of holding whatever needs to be held.

We also all have everyday experiences of containers that are more meaningful and rich: the bottle of wine we shared with our beloved on our first date, the urn we find for our father-in-law's ashes, the velveteen-covered box that a beautiful piece of gifted jewelry sits in, the pens we use to write with ink on paper, jars of paint ready for art-making, that tube of talismanic lip-stick, a golden locket carrying the picture of our mother and a tiny flower we once gave her, and those hand-blown bottles of perfume we keep on our vanity. Our containers span the range from banal plastic tubs to fine crystal and gold. And like our relationship with water, our relationship with containers and the act of being held begins long before we draw our first breath, when we are contained inside the watery womb, and continues when we, as little children (if we are so fortunate), are held by the strong and loving arms of someone who cares.

As we are held, we also learn to hold. We contain ourselves: the essence of our breath, the bright spark of mind and eye, the warm beats of heart, and the dancing swirl of blood. Our throats and mouths contain speech, our eyes hold vision, our nose is a sacred vessel for scent just as our ears are for sound. When it comes to our physicality in the world, most of us do not hold things perfectly. A sense here or there is damaged. We constantly forget to breathe as deeply or slowly or clearly as we should. And yet, at the end of the day, it all works well enough. So we remember that, like all magic, our ways of holding don't have to be perfect. The chipped bowl can still function, the cracked cup still carry clean water.

In our exploration of containers, we first must realize that we actually need them, make use of them, and rely upon them. Once we begin to see that clearly, we can then consider what containers we make the *most* use of. Do you have a favorite cup or bowl that you find yourself picking out again and again? What makes it special? What product packaging draws your eye and brings sensual pleasure, and why does it appeal so? What kinds of containers make you wrinkle your nose in dislike? Do you abhor plastic and instead find yourself seeking out containers made of natural materials that can easily biodegrade? Are you smitten with vessels covered in retro art and made of old-fashioned materials? Do you prefer lots of smaller containers as opposed to large ones? Do you like containers that are left open to the air, like vases and bowls, or do you prefer those with lids and tops? Are there kinds of containers that feel especially magical and extraordinary to you? Are there particular containers that you hold dear, such as decoupage boxes containing old sets of tarot cards or the nice fountain pen you received on your thirteenth birthday? Begin to notice what containers you work with every day, as well as what kinds of containers you tend to avoid.

Consider also what your preferred containers hold. Office supplies like pencils and paper clips? Pantry staples like sugar and salt? Strong coffee? Cold milk? Honey? Expensive perfumes or magical oils? Cosmetics? Jewelry? Tobacco? Do you have terra cotta pots filled with sharply scented green herbs and loamy soil? Flowers full of bees and pollen? Bird nests that hold eggs and the promise of new life? Maybe your favorite containers are the ones that house your talismans and treasures.

The kinds of containers that appeal to you *and* the things that are held best by these containers each have the capacity to speak directly to the ways in which you might magically work with sacred vessels. Looking at what we hold and how we hold it in our daily lives often gives us a clue about what we need to hold and how we need to hold it within the extraordinary as well.

RITUAL FIRST CUP OF THE DAY

Most of us begin our days with a sacred vessel for our ubiquitous morning beverages, whatever they happen to be—coffee, hot water and lemon, a steaming cup of tea. This ritual makes good use of those first cups of the morning and helps us start our day off right.

TIME   5 to 10 minutes

MATERIALS
- ~ your Making Magic journal
- ~ your first beverage of the day
- ~ a door (optional)
- ~ a special talisman (optional)
- ~ candles (optional)
- ~ incense (optional)

PROCESS
Perform the "Easy Breath Relax and Release" from chapter 2. Open your door; touch your talisman, sharing with it your desire for this ritual; and light your candles or incense, as you like.

Take some time to consider what you want to hold space for today. This might be a specific situation. You may need to hold space for a loved one who has to give their companion animal a good death or a difficult colleague at work who needs support.

You may need to hold space for yourself as you have a tricky conversation or decide to go against the grain and just rest.

Once you have a sense of who or what you want to hold space for, write it down in your Making Magic journal. You also might want to make a little prayer or petition with it and recite it over your beverage.

As you are ready, breathe your blessing over the beverage.

Drink up the beverage in one big gulp or in little sips.

Once you have finished your beverage, breathe in a blessing and exhale in gratitude. You are now holding space.

FIELD NOTES FROM THE EXTRAORDINARY

Given our intimate and ongoing relationship to containers and the various ways of holding space, it is only sensible that we would make magic around the concept of containers and sacred vessels. An eggshell that has had the yolk blown out and is filled with confetti, glitter, and petition papers; a copper bowl inscribed with a petition that swirls down to its base; a vase holding flowers that have been left as an offering on an altar; a jar brimming over with honey and the just-right words and roots to sweeten a love relationship or to persuade a friend to forgive harsh words that were never meant; a box full of sparkling stones and cash, designed to attract and draw more prosperity into your life; or the knothole of an old tree holding a simple offering of acorns and flowers made to the spirits of the land—all containers, all sacred vessels, all magic.

The extraordinary qualities of everyday containers tell us what kinds of magic-making they are best at supporting. Because containers hold things—literally containing them, holding space—working with containers is a natural thing to do whenever we need to make something more stable or cohesive. Because containers can hold a number of different objects or substances, we may find that situations that have many moving parts are easy to address through the use of a magical container. And because objects and places to put them are concepts that young children intuitively grasp, creating magical containers with our little ones is a beautiful way to introduce them to their own magic.

Just as a little treasure is transformed into a talisman or the coffee we brew every morning becomes the first potion of our day, so too our ways of holding speak simultaneously to the practical and magical aspects of our lives.

How do you need to hold or contain a specific situation, desire, goal, or want? What in your desires and goals needs to be given proper boundaries and delineation? What needs to be excluded and kept out or removed from your concerns? What needs to be included, protected, and shielded? What elements are vulnerable and in need of strong walls and supports? What qualities need to be contained but not completely covered up? What kind of sacred vessel is the best for holding a particular work? A clear glass jar? A handcrafted pottery vase? A rattle made of twine and rawhide and filled with pumpkin seeds? A hollowed-out apple that can be filled with honey and buried at the foot of a tree? A blue sphere filled with pins and needles and sparkles that can be hung from the window and used to trap any negative thoughts, habits, or spirits that may try to make their way into your sacred space? The world of containers is incredibly varied, so when we begin to work with these vessels in a magical context, we do well to take our time and think about what the just-right vessel is to hold our particular kind of magic.

In the same way you ask how a situation, goal, or desire needs to be held, you must also ask what the best way of holding it is. Are you dealing with a scenario where a little more sweetness and kindness would go a long way? Then perhaps whatever else you do, you need to include some sugar or honey in your containers. Are you working on a situation that requires fresh thinking and new perspective? What botanical allies have you started forming a relationship with that might be just right for that job? Are you creating a sacred vessel to honor a specific holy helper? If so, what substances are strongly associated with them? Your sacred vessels might be filled with water left in the moonlight, white wine, champagne, raw brown sugar, golden honey, multicolored seeds and beans, dried flowers and strong roots, living plants and rich earth, rice for luck and money, or scraps of paper inscribed with blessing and petition, sign and symbol, and all topped off with glitter.

However elaborate or simple you make a sacred vessel, after creating it, there is one more set of questions to ask, and these deal with how you work with your sacred vessel in an ongoing manner. Again, begin with where you are and consider the situation, want, desire, or need that your magical container is addressing. What needs to happen with your situation or concern, your desire or need, in order for there to be resolution and completion? Do you want to position your sacred vessel in a place where you can see it on a daily basis? You may want to pray over it, inscribe its outside with petitions, or light a candle in front of it or on top of it and allow the wax to gently warm it up, encouraging movement. Perhaps you need to shake your sacred vessel rhythmically, breathe over it, sing over it, or speak over it. You may find that you want to internalize the intentions you have imbued your magical container with so that you use its contents in your cooking or the seasoning of food. Do you feel the need to place your magical container in a significant spot? The bowl of potpourri at the entrance to your front door may have more than one purpose; the gratitude jar on your dining room table can exert its subtle influence through all mealtimes. Or maybe you need to bury your container at the base of a tree for good health or at the line of a threshold for protection and house blessing. Or maybe you need to throw it into the depths of a river so that whatever negative habit you are releasing will sink to the bottom of the deep waters.

Just as the ingredients found in our pantries and cupboards are often called on to perform double or triple duty—as sources of food, medicine, and magic—the same is true of sacred vessels. The sugar in the canister on our counter is used in baking and sweetening our coffee or tea; it can also be called upon to create more sweetness in the home.

Though the world of sacred vessels and magical containers is wide and varied, as always, we begin with what we already know and have. So consider the containers you use every day, multiple times a day, and ask how those might be put to extraordinary, magical use right alongside their everyday functions. Here is a little ritual that gives one suggestion on how to do that.

RITUAL A SACRED SALTCELLAR

This ritual teaches you how to create a very simple magical container with your saltcellar. Salt is a mineral that has long been associated with both purification and protection. Adding salt to food and cooking is something most of us do numerous times a day, so the way of working with this particular sacred vessel is by taking its blessing into our bodies and replenishing its contents whenever we need to. Finely chopped dried onion, garlic, or chives may be added to the salt to increase its qualities of protection and also to add savor and richness to its flavor. If you responsibly wildcraft these ingredients or harvest them from your garden, then you will make magic on several different levels at the same time and improve your relationship to the land where you live. Rice is used to keep salt grains separated and dried and is especially useful in humid climates, but rice is also considered a luck- and wealth-drawing staple in many cultures.

TIME   15 to 20 minutes

MATERIALS
- ~ your Making Magic journal
- ~ salt (you may use sea salt, kosher salt, regular table salt—whatever you like)
- ~ a few grains of rice—again, any kind will do
- ~ a pinch of finely chopped dried onion, garlic, or chives (optional)
- ~ a small bowl
- ~ a container for the salt—either a saltcellar or a salt grinder

PROCESS
Perform the "Easy Breath Relax and Release" from chapter 2.

Take some time to consider what in your life and in the lives of the people you live with needs to be held safe, stable, protected, and pure. Once you have a sense of those qualities, you can write them down in your Making Magic journal.

As you are ready, take the salt, breathe in a blessing over it, exhale in gratitude, and pour it into a small bowl.

Next, take some time to consider what in your life and in the lives of the people you live with needs to be blessed with good luck, good fortune, and the blessings of prosperity. Once you have a sense of those qualities, you can write them down in your Making Magic journal.

As you are ready, take the rice, breathe in a blessing over it, exhale in gratitude, and add it to the salt.

Then take some time to consider what in your life and in the lives of the people you live with needs to be protected, enriched, and enlivened. Once you have a sense of those qualities, you can write them down in your Making Magic journal.

As you are ready, take the optional chopped and dried onion, garlic, or chives, breathe in a blessing over them, exhale in gratitude, and add these ingredients to the salt and rice.

Stir the contents of the bowl three times in a clockwise manner so that they are well mixed. As you stir them together, keep in mind your goal for this magical salt and bless it so that all who use it to season their food and cooking are able to experience the blessings it carries.

Once you have finished, breathe in one more blessing, exhaling in gratitude, and then add the salt to the saltcellar or salt grinder. Congratulations! You now have a practical and magical sacred vessel fit for daily use.

Final act: When your salt starts to run low, repeat the ritual as needed, and experiment with different ingredients that you can add to your salt for more refined magic-making.

STEPPING STONES

- Your belly is also a sacred vessel. Take a deep breath and fill your belly with air. How does it feel when it is full? Exhale completely. How does it feel when it is empty?

- Sweeten your home fast by adding three whole vanilla pods to your sugar canister. The vanilla will infuse your sugar with warmth, and every time you add sugar to any recipe, everyone in your home will be warmed up too!

- Identify a container you use all of the time. For me it is my pencil and pen jar. Anoint it with some oil or cense it with a favorite sacred smoke and a specific petition. Notice what happens as you use the container and its contents. Do you feel the effects of your magic?

There are many magical stories about sacred vessels that can magically produce without end: the horn of plenty, bottomless beakers full of mead that never run dry, cauldrons that produce enough porridge to feed a starving family or fill up a cottage. In each tale, the emphasis is on the boundless generosity each sacred vessel expresses—and on our ability to make best and wisest use of that generosity. At bottom, this is the remembered magic of sacred vessels: a reminder that our inner resources are limitless when they are held strong by good walls and good boundaries.

13

SMOKE AND FIRE

A great flame follows a little spark.

DANTE ALIGHIERI, *The Divine Comedy* (Charles S. Singleton, translator)[1]

Wherever we live and whatever our experiences of our land-scapes, both inner and outer, when night falls over us and the terrain of our soul soil is cloaked in darkness, we call upon a singular element to help us see, to guide us on, to keep us safe and warm, and to nourish us, through the cooking of food and the illuminating of shadows. We call on fire.

The last trial in the pursuit of our *own* magic is a trial by fire. Among its other virtues, fire is physically and magically used to test and to assay, to determine what components a specific object might be made of, to allow us to truly see our mettle, to discern the true from the false, and to get it just right. It is no coincidence that in the story of "Golden Locks and the Three Bears," the first place where Golden Locks is tested is at the bears' hearth. If she cannot pass that first test, then she will not make it to the next, and as we discover, getting it just right is as much about calling upon our inner fire, in the form of determination and passion, as it is about any knowledge or training we may or may not have received. And so magic teaches: pass through the fires of life by cultivating, stoking, and feeding the fires within.

In this chapter, we will examine our relationships to fire—inner and outer, everyday and extraordinary—discovering in the process how and why this element is so often viewed as the embodiment of magic.

FIELD NOTES FROM THE EVERYDAY

We strike a match into luminous flame. We light candles to scent our homes, grace our tables, create romantic mood lighting in our bedrooms, and lull our little ones to sleep. We flick on the burners on our stovetop to prepare a meal, and flames rise up or electric coils heat up with their own inner fire. We sweat it out—at the gym, during our morning run, through a sequence of yoga poses, or as we garden under the hot sun, creating the inner fire that the Hindu tradition refers to as *tapas*. We pile into our cars and turn the ignition so that the combustion begins to take form and shape, creating motion and movement where before all was still. Our foods are spiced with chilies, peppers, and pungent ingredients like onions, garlic, and ginger, creating a culinary fire on our tongues. And we hold our lovers in entwined embraces celebrating and honoring the fire of burning passion. These are just some of the ways that the element of fire, like that of water, shows up in our lives on a daily basis.

Every sunrise reminds us of the fact that each day is circumscribed by an arc of blazing fire. Fire arouses. It ignites. Fire transforms. Not a fluid, solid, or aerial element, it inhabits

its own form, seeking out fuel, casting forth light, calling us into movement, contemplation, warmth, and vision. For eons, flame and sacred smoke were found at the center of great ceremonies and small rituals. Centuries later they were safeguarded in the hearths of homes, rarely or never allowed to go out. As the divisions between the everyday and the extraordinary have grown, and the ruptures between us and Creation have removed certain realities from our field of vision, we have found ways to shield ourselves from the central role that fire plays in our lives. And that makes sense, for all of the old stories about fire and those who loved it, like the story of Prometheus, warn us of this element's double-edged nature: it can create, but it can also destroy. We are surrounded by this element, and so it is our task to come into right relationship with it, beginning as always with our everyday experience.

What is the role that fire plays in your life right here and right now? Begin with the outer forms. Do you love candles? Lanterns? Is a fire in the fireplace during cold winter months a necessity from your point of view? Do you prefer outdoor fires, made in the woods and surrounded by friends or family? Is it the fire of hearth that appeals to you most, allowing you to take raw ingredients and alchemically transform them into something nourishing and satisfying? The fire of electricity that powers up your laptop and keeps your devices charged allows you to sink into a favorite book even though it is the middle of the night—where does that electricity come from? What fuels the fires you experience on a daily basis? Is it the power of flame to heat water, warm skin, cauterize a wound that feels most essential to you? How do you get fired up? Do you hit the gym and stir up the flames in skin and muscle and sweat? Do you literally bring fire into your body by eating spicy foods or drinking hot beverages? Do you connect with the fire of the sun or the radiance of the moon? Where and how does fire show up in your daily life?

One of the unique properties of fire is that while it illuminates certain spaces, it also, through that illumination, allows us to see shadows. As Ursula K. Le Guin describes it, "To light a candle is to cast a shadow."[2] This is physically true and, like all physical truths, carries a deeper resonance as well—one that inspires ritual.

RITUAL SHADOW PLAY

This tiny ritual makes use of something many of us do on a daily basis—lighting a candle.

TIME 5 to 10 minutes

MATERIALS
- ~ your Making Magic journal
- ~ candle—any kind will do
- ~ a door (optional)
- ~ a special talisman (optional)
- ~ incense (optional)

PROCESS
Perform the "Easy Breath Relax and Release" from chapter 2. Open your door; touch your talisman, sharing with it your desire for this ritual; and light your incense, as you like.

Light the candle. Sit or stand back and allow yourself to watch it burn. Notice the light that it casts and notice too what shadows show up when the candle is lit.

Take some time to reflect on the relationship between light and shadow. What do you see physically happening as your candle burns? What does that relationship teach you about your own light and shadow? Write your reflections in your Making Magic journal.

Feel free to build upon the work we have done in previous chapters and ask the burning flame what it wants you to know, how it wants to be incorporated into your life, what medicines it might hold for you. As always, note the answers in your Making Magic journal.

When you are ready, you may snuff or blow the flame out. If you blow it out, do so with the intention of blowing forward the good work you have done—into the rest of your day, into the rest of your life.

Breathe in a blessing on yourself. Exhale in gratitude.

✳

FIELD NOTES FROM THE EXTRAORDINARY

Our relationship with fire, flame, and smoke is, like all of our remembered magic, both an inner and outer one. There are the candles and the campfires, hearth fires and bonfires, that grace our lives at various times and seasons. And then there is the fire that burns within each of us. The deepest light is found burning at our core, just as the earth's hot, molten core is beneath our feet.

This inner fire is understood to be the first spark of life, and the light that radiates out from it is understood to be the source of all other life that revolves out from and around it. It is the pulsing, beating, sacred heart. It is the clot of blood that, in Iroquois creation myth, is spun faster and faster by old, tricky Hare.[3] It is the glowing *agni* of Hindu tradition.[4] It is the sacred fire venerated by the ancient Greeks.[5] It is the Holy Spirit honored by Christians. Its crackling embers remind us that however broken, scarred, and wounded we may feel, and whatever hellish experiences and stories we have known, there is at the root of each of us something that is utterly indestructible, whose purpose is to burn and burnish, illuminating our shadows, revealing the bright gold that has always been present in the veins of our soul's bedrock.

Traditions the world over teach that this personal flame cannot be vanquished, but it can be threatened. Much as the absence of water in our inner lives can be noticed, so too can the absence of fire. Without the warmth and presence of our inner spark, we show up tired, exhausted, "burned out," depleted, and low energy. When we feel a lack of enthusiasm (*enthusiasm* literally meaning "to be filled with God"), when we are unable to be generous or warm or loving, and when we experience moments of feeling frozen, paralyzed, not knowing or really much caring what might happen next, then we know that our inner flames have banked dangerously low. And just as water is essential to growth, fertility, fecundity, and life, so is fire. We know that the sun's glowing flames reach far into space—far enough to touch our own sphere, far enough to keep us warm and turn the plants green and allow for the possibility of all growth and all life. We know from our own bouncing blood vessel and beating heart and bright eye that there is no life without the burning flame.

So look inward, touching the extraordinary. What is the state of your inner fire? Are you bright and burning? Is your inner fire too strong, devouring fuel faster than you can provide it? Is it banked too low? Do you find yourself having a hard time getting excited, opening the way for wonder and curiosity to illuminate your path? Do you feel lackluster? Too cold? Frozen in place? Unable to move? Do you burn steady? Do you share your warmth, brightness, and generosity with others, or do you hoard it all to yourself in a contained, sharp flame? What fuels that inner fire? What fuel allows your sparks to burn ever brighter? What feeds your ability to be warm, enthusiastic, generous, and passionate? Books, good art, make-out sessions with your lover, swims in deep pools of rock and water, walks in the woods, lounging with your cat, stargazing, divining with tarot cards, making soup, laughter that we can't stop, the tears that we finally need to shed—all are potential sources of fuel, and there are so very many more. What are yours?

Throughout time fire has been regarded as a highly magical element for so many of its qualities. Chief among them are its ability to burn and in so doing to transform, utterly and completely, something from one state into another. In science class, we learned that this transformation is referred to as a chemical change, but in our deep remembering, we know it as making magic. Fire's ability to illuminate and burn away what is no longer needed is connected to its long use throughout magic as a force for both blessing and protection. Circles made of fire have the power to keep away all kinds of threats. Even today great bonfires are built in order to confer protection on the people and animals who dare to leap through their flames, and calling on the subtle inner fire of spices like black pepper and red chilies is a time-honored way to remove negative influences, situations, or people from our lives.

As we remember our magic, we remember too the deeper nature of fire, and we begin to recognize the various ways we may be able to work with it. Contemplate your goals and desires, needs and wants; home in and listen deeply to the sound of your *telos* singing through you. What needs to be illuminated in these areas? What needs light cast onto the shadows? What needs to be brightened? Are there areas where you feel that your vision may be obscured? Places that feel opaque or uncertain? Paths that cannot be traversed safely or at all without some kind of guiding light? What about a given situation or concern needs to be transformed? What elements might need to be burned away completely, removed from the scenario, rendered into ash? What notions or compulsions are you ready to see clearly and then incinerate?

Transformation, as the alchemists of old promised, works in both directions. Fire can destroy, but it can also reveal. So ask too, What needs to be revealed? What needs to be refined? What gold is ready to be revealed, strengthened, and reinforced? What in a given situation may need to be warmed, hurried up, set into motion, or thawed out? Cold hearts, frigid words, icy relationships—all can benefit from the warmth of fire.

The fuel that a fire is given in everyday life determines much about the nature of the fire. How bright and fast a fire burns, the scents and aromas that rise up from it, and even the quality of its ash, all speak to the kinds of fuel that were provided. Many fires are made extraordinary through the use of the right fuel. Sacred woods and leaves, herbs, and resins lead to equally sacred and fragrant smoke that we can work with to cleanse, purify, and cense objects, places, and people, bestowing airborne blessings. What are the fuels in your situations and scenarios? What is feeding your goals and dreams, desires and needs? Are the fuels plentiful and able to yield the right kind of fire, or are they too paltry or more likely to lead to explosive flames instead of a consistent and steady burn?

We can make magic with flame and smoke in a variety of ways, from lighting some incense to building fires, learning to tend them, gazing into them, and learning from them. But the most beloved way to honor fire in our rituals is through the lighting of a simple candle—something many of us often do—which once again elicits the extraordinary from within the deep interstices of the everyday.

RITUAL RELEASE AND REVITALIZE CANDLE RITE

This is a ritual that is designed to melt away whatever aspects from your situation are no longer needed, while at the same time stoking the flames and vitality of the aspects you do want to strengthen and support.

TIME At least 10 minutes, but it really depends on the size of the candle you work with.

MATERIALS
- ~ your Making Magic journal
- ~ a candle—any kind you want, from a birthday cake candle to a lovely scented candle from your favorite gift shop (I do recommend a new candle that has not been used before.)
- ~ a door (optional)
- ~ a special talisman (optional)
- ~ incense (optional)

PROCESS
Perform the "Easy Breath Relax and Release" from chapter 2. Open your door; touch your talisman, sharing with it your desire for this ritual; and light your incense, as you like.

Consider a situation that is pressing on you at this time. What about the situation needs to melt away? Note your answers in your Making Magic journal.

Next, consider what elements of the situation need to be illuminated and revitalized. What needs to be fired up? Note these answers in your Making Magic journal as well.

Attending to the answers you gave to the questions above, breathe in a blessing on yourself and your work, and exhale in gratitude.

Light the candle. Affirm that as the wax melts, whatever needs to melt away from your situation also does so. Affirm that as the fire burns, whatever needs to be brightened and strengthened in your situation also is.

Allow the candle to burn all the way through, or breathe in a blessing and then blow or snuff it out in gratitude and relight it the next day.

Once the candle has finished burning, assess your situation. What has moved and changed about it? How has this most simple fire transformed it?

Breathe in a blessing on the work that you have done. Exhale in gratitude.

STEPPING STONES

- Reflect on what the best sources of fuel are for you personally. How often do you have access to them? When are they available? What practical actions can you take to emphasize them in your daily life?

- In many traditions, stoking our inner fire is viewed as a merit-creating act. You can then dedicate those merits to a specific endeavor. For example, choose a physical activity you want to do, like exercising, gardening, or even simple stretching. Before you engage in the activity, dedicate the merits of your work to something close to your heart, such as a nonprofit whose work inspires you.

- To make infused fire water, take a glass
  jar full of water and set it outside during
  sunrise. Leave it there until high noon,
  when the sun is at its zenith. Then drink it
  down. Notice how you feel afterward.

At the end of "Purgatorio," Dante—the hero who has literally gone through hell—has the opportunity to make it to heaven, to Paradise. There is only one catch: he has to walk through a wall of flame. Magic demands this of us too. Every time we create a ceremony, every time we perform a ritual, we are calling on the transformative powers of the cosmos, and chief among them is that of fire. We can and do transform our outer situations but only when we have the bravery and fiery heart courage to transform our inner lives too. As we remember our own magic, we come closer and closer to those walls of flame. They challenge us even now. Are we ready to take the final steps?

14

WEAVING THE WORLDS
BACK TOGETHER

A meandering line sutures together the world
in some new way, as though walking was sewing
and sewing was telling a story and that story was your life.
REBECCA SOLNIT, *The Faraway Nearby*[1]

The way to seek out, call for, and remember deep magic is simple: take a walk through the wilds of your soul soil, while reflecting on your everyday experience. You may never have imagined that the everyday could be so endlessly interesting and full of hidden possibilities and surprises, that it could be so extraordinary. Nowhere else can the unseen be seen and the unrealized become possible. The wild beating heart of magic was never very far away from life to begin with.

Stopping at a stoplight on the way to work, picking up lunch for the crew, walking the dog, sweeping up the floor—no matter how small or apparently mundane daily acts are, each one is an opportunity for mending the broken places, bridging the chasms, weaving the world of the everyday and the extraordinary into each other again and anew. As you near the end of your journey, you can now see that you have been engaging in magical acts without even realizing it. This, then, is the fundamental work of magic: to realize what has already been happening, to gain the sense of it. And by doing so, we find that the magical potency of everyday life is drawn out like a fruit from its flower. Now we can stand with strength in both worlds, seeing and embracing all sides and aspects, bringing all sides of soul and experience to the star-laden table of the cosmos—including and especially the parts that are still wild, still unknown, that elude our grasp ever and always.

Finally, all the elements of experience are ready to be woven together. The Fates with their spindle and woolen threads; the Norns with their bone needles and sinew strings; and Tse-Che-Nako, Spider Grandmother of the Pueblo peoples, with her silks—they are all weavers, and that is exactly what is needed. Spinning and weaving are some of the oldest crafts, work of the hands that literally makes culture possible. This is one reason they have been used throughout the world as a metaphor for not just how we live life but also how Creation itself came to be. It is why weaving, as practical skill, as metaphor, and as magic, has accompanied people through human history.

In our guiding tale, the heroine undergoes a change. She transforms from sweet, innocent, childlike Golden Locks into Headstrong and Heartstrong Woman, for she has found what she was seeking, and in so doing, she wove herself back together as well. She wove herself back together with the Bear People, back together with Creation, back together with her magic. She wove the world of everyday and the realm of the extraordinary back into each other once more. So it is for us as well. And so it is that spinning, weaving, threading, and sewing magic is some of the most ancient. It is often one of the aspects of magic that we remember last, although it is ever present for us. Once magic is remembered, and memory is recovered, we too are given the privilege and responsibility of weaving the worlds back together once more. No matter who we are, where we come from, what station in life we find ourselves in, or what challenges we have been asked to meet, this is our gift.

Our exploration of this oldest of old arts begins by contemplating the cloth that covers the whole of human life—clothing and garments. From there, the inquiry proceeds deep into the warp and weft of things, seeking out the magic and embracing it once more.

FIELD NOTES FROM THE EVERYDAY

After we awaken, one of the first things we do is put on clothes in readiness for the day. A morning change of garments marks the transition from sleeping to waking life. For some of us, this is a delightfully sensual experience of going into an organized closet, sorting through fabric, material, and color until we assemble the just-right outfit. For others, it is a chore; we may even find ourselves digging through piles of clothes on the floor—some clean, some dirty—or scanning the offerings in the closet until we discover whatever is clean enough to work for the day.

We all have strong preferences about clothing, whether we know it or not. Even the man who claims that he cares nothing about clothes cares deeply. What he is saying is that he is very discerning about his clothing: he wants *this* kind of shirt from that sort of retail store and that costs X amount of dollars, and no other kind.

Textures, materials, colors, and cuts matter. Placed over sensitive skin, clothing not only conceals but also reveals—that is, it performs the function of displaying something of our personality to the world. In countries and among peoples who have very little in the ways of resources, gorgeous fabrics and materials abound. Clothing garments are like our physical spaces: they surround us at all times, for hour upon hour. The notion that magical potency might be discovered here is not at all far-fetched.

Clothing is so intimate to life that an examination of the subject can stir up knots of frustration and shame. For those of us who have grown up influenced by the Judeo-Christian tradition and its stories, the origin of clothing is found in the story of the first people's shame of having done something against a jealous god's wishes. There is timeless truth in this old story: the act of covering up by means of clothing is still, for many of us, an expression of body shame or self-protection. The question of clothing touches upon deeply interwoven attitudes about money, reputation, aspiration, fears and hopes, neglect and care, our sense of self and self-worth, and attitudes about body, soul, and mind. In the same way treasures and talismans allow us to name broken places and the blessings that emerge from them, so does reflecting on our most basic attitudes about clothing.

Begin anywhere. What clothes do you currently have that you actually like? Maybe there is only one item. If so, then this is where you start. Include accessories like scarves and wraps, veils and shoes. Pick out one item. What do you like about it? How does it make you feel when you wear it? Where do you like to wear it? Is there anything about it you don't like or would change? If so, what?

Expand this out beyond the clothes that you wear. Look through all of the fabrics you have—in your closet and in your home. We are surrounded by all kinds of fabrics—from sheets, pillows, and towels, to carpets, curtains, and furniture upholstery. What textures feel good to you? What colors are naturally resonant, and what are not? Do you love double-piled velvets and soft wools, plain and simple white cotton, or silks and satins? Do you appreciate fabrics with some internal structure that are a bit stiffer and crisp, or do you want only the softest things to touch your skin? Are you a fan of prints or artisan-dyed textiles, or do you like clean lines and minimal fuss?

Like doors, houses, containers, and the elements of water and fire, fabric is ubiquitous in human life. It need not be fancy or expensive in order to be special. Like all of the everyday objects and concepts worked with throughout this book, fabric is an everyday material that admits in every crease and fold the extraordinary.

RITUAL HEALING TOUCH

Fabric can literally and magically be used to conceal and protect; it can also be used to heal. This is a small ritual that relies on fabric to facilitate healing at the mental, spiritual, emotional, or spiritual level. It comes from ancient customs found throughout Europe, especially England, Ireland, and Scotland, and was brought into the Americas by those who emigrated from these countries. In the original context, the cloth used is called a *cloutie*.

TIME   1 hour

MATERIALS

~ your Making Magic journal

~ a piece of natural cloth or fabric about as big as the palm of your hand

~ the person who is requesting healing, whether that is you or someone else

~ a good, healthy tree to hang the cloth in at the end of the ritual

~ a door (optional)

~ a special talisman (optional)

~ incense (optional)

PROCESS

Perform the "Easy Breath Release and Relax" from chapter 2. Open your door; touch your talisman, sharing with it your desire for this ritual; and light your incense, as you like.

Speak to the person who is requesting healing. Ask what kind of healing they are in need of and where it hurts. Listen to their/your responses. If you are doing this ritual for yourself, you may want to ask the question and record the response in your Making Magic journal.

Apply the cloth to the place that hurts. In a physical healing situation, this will be easy. If you are dealing with healing that needs to happen on an emotional, spiritual, or mental level, it might be more complicated, but by this point you know how to think about it. Someone who feels anxious and worried all the time would need their head to be touched by the cloth. Someone who feels creatively stymied might need their hands touched by the cloth. Someone who is heartbroken will need to have their chest come into contact with the cloth.

As you hold the cloth to the afflicted place, have the individual breathe in a blessing for themselves and then exhale whatever disease and affliction they wish to release.

Take the cloth and hang it on a healthy, living tree. If you can hang it on a tree that is by a natural body of water, even better.

Affirm and acknowledge that as the cloth disintegrates and is taken off by creatures and the natural elements, so too the illness will be carried away.

Breathe in a blessing on your work. Exhale in gratitude.

✳

A good follow-up to this rite is a sacred bath, either for yourself or the person you performed the ritual for (see chapter 11).

FIELD NOTES FROM THE EXTRAORDINARY

Every component that goes into the creation of fabric speaks to the presence of the extraordinary. Weaving is the foundation for all fabric, and all weaving begins with spinning. Spinning relies on rhythmic circular motion and brings order to chaos. And whether you think through the pages of a book by Aristotle, take the hero's journey with Dante, listen to the creation stories of the Navajo or the Iroquois people, you will find that all of them tell you the same thing: bringing order to chaos is how the world began. This is how creation started: by the earth spinning, on the axis, around the sun; by one cell spinning into two. Even now, at this moment, our blood cells continue weaving together their first miracle, the blessed body.

Wool, silk, stories, life experiences—whatever material we start out with sits there in our laps and in a tangle. And so we collect it, little by little, snarl by snarl. We gather up the tangles and work it around the distaff, the spindle, with our hands and later with the powerful force of a spinning wheel. The wheel's regular, rhythmic, circular motion soon brings thread into creation. Now there is something distinct: a *one*. Now there is something that has come out of the chaotic tangle that is deeply useful. For thread can be used to tie down and make strong. It can be called on to measure, and so the possibility of culture, balance, and ratio is born. Thread, above all, can be woven together with other thread. And then all is possible: protection, shelter, strength, beauty, and story. *From the one, two, and from two, the limitless.*

The acts of sewing and weaving have also been the perfect place to hide. It may stun us to realize how resilient magic is, how hidden it has needed to be, in order to survive for so long. Its survival has depended on self-protective coloration, just like the survival of any species that has been hunted, persecuted, burned alive, not once but many, many times. And still to have made it, for the old rootstock under the charred earth not to have completely given up the ghost—that is something special. How did magic do it?

It happened in many ways, but one of the ways was with the weavers, the sewers, quilters, and cloth makers—the circles of women who came together to do their "women's work" of sewing and spinning and quilting and darning. Who knows what was said in those private circles, away from men and away, most especially, from the dominant religious forms? What secrets were safeguarded? What sacred arts were watered and fed and nourished just enough, by tough hands, tender glances, and secret smiles so that they had the strength to sustain for another day? Sewing circle, magic circle—not so very different.

The magic of warp and weft, cloth and knot, is there for anyone to remember too. Start with what you know, see, and experience in the everyday. Think about the cloth, fabric, and clothes that you know best, and consider your own needs and wants, desires, and deep *telos*. What needs to be covered? What needs to be shielded or protected? What needs to be hidden? What needs to be revealed? What is ready to be displayed ornately in order to draw attention to itself, to seduce, to beguile? What wishes to be tucked up, gathered in, veiled, and wrapped up in either loose or tight folds? Where do the colors need to be more vibrant or demure? What is ready to be seen once and for all?

Think and feel into the process of making fabric and cloth. You may be an old hat at sewing and cloth handcrafts, or you may not know anything about them. It doesn't matter, for the components are universal: needle, thread, knots.

Take the needle. What in your life, your goals and dreams, your needs and wants, requires piercing? What has grown too inflated, too puffed up? What has taken on a life larger than its own? What molehills have been turned into mountains? Pierce them and be sharp about it, deflating and bringing them back to the ground, where they can be made useful once more. What forces may need to be poked and prodded into action—or into staying away and giving you space? Where might you need to snag yourself or someone else in order to create time and space for needle-sharp, sword-sharp discernment? What might you need to literally or figuratively *pin* down?

Move to thread. What loose threads need to be gathered in and gathered up? Can you create something new from them, or are they better off soaked in sacred water and hung in the trees for the birds to build nests with? What are the through lines and through threads running across your concern or desire? What are the themes you return to again and again? Where does good, red thread need to be laid down in the dusty street to guide you home and out of the Minotaur's labyrinth? Where do parts of a story or relationships you cherish or your own understanding of self and Creation need to be sewn together, tightly bound, made stronger, made durable?

Now reflect on and work with knots. What are the knots currently present in your life, and how might you best untangle them? Do they need to be cut through with a sharp sword or picked apart with a needle? Should they be untangled or allowed to stay fixed until the way through is clear? What in your life, in the situations and relationships that occupy you, most needs to be tied down, knotted back into place, or set free and loosened to fly in the winds?

Remember too that knots are used for counting, for praying, for keeping rhythm and cycles of sacred time. What needs to be remembered and recalled, touched upon, when it comes to your own rhythms, your own sense of sacred time, your own best devotions?

Weave it together. Where do different threads, different parts of self, different parts of story need to be woven into one another once more or for the first time, so that they form a whole? You have been weaving throughout this entire book as you remember your own magic. You have been walking through your wild lands and weaving your own best sense of what is needed and required, right here and right now, into what is possible and good and necessary. You have been weaving the blessings in and out of your own broken places, weaving the everyday directly into the extraordinary.

Ask too where things need to be unwoven. What has been too entwined and enmeshed for far too long? What attitudes, woven into your everyday life from who knows when and who knows where, are you finally ready to untangle and separate? Weaving makes use of all of the above: needle and thread and knot, warp and weft. What are the places in your own life where all resources need to be called together in order to surround yourself with something not only extraordinary but also lasting? What other sacred arts are you now ready to weave into your ability to make magic?

RITUAL WORKING OUT THE KNOTS

This little ritual is well known in my city. The version that I was
taught originates with the *currendera* healing traditions of the
American Southwest and Mexico. This ceremony is one that I was
taught by some of my elders and is an excellent precursor to actual
bodywork, specifically massage or hands-on healing.

TIME   15 to 30 minutes

MATERIALS

- ~ your Making Magic journal
- ~ a piece of red thread, yarn, or string
  about as long as your forearm
- ~ a fire-safe container (optional)
- ~ matches (optional)
- ~ a door (optional)
- ~ a talisman (optional)
- ~ incense (optional)

PROCESS

Perform the "Easy Breath Relax and Release" from chapter 2.
Open your door; touch your talisman, sharing with it your desire
for this ritual; and light your incense, as you like.

Affirm and acknowledge that you are going to perform a
ceremony of working out the knots.

Take some time to consider what the major current stresses
in your life are. These are stresses that show up for you every
day, create a great deal of anxiety, and prevent you from clearly
focusing. They may be practical, emotional, physical; everyone's
list is different. Write them down in your Making Magic journal.

Go over the list and notice if there are any that do not
feel especially serious or acute. If there are, eliminate them

from your list. Once you are ready with your list, create a petition that you can say aloud during the ceremony.

You may write your own petition or use this form: "Dear/ Blessed/Beloved [insert name of your chosen holy helper or helpers], I come to you as [state your full name], tied up with the following concerns, stresses, and anxieties [state the concerns, anxieties, and worries that you wish to unravel], so that I may be in ever deeper alignment with [name your *telos*]."

For each worry, anxiety, or concern you listed, make a knot in the thread.

After you have done this, you have a couple of options. One is to take the knotted thread, ritually burn it in a fire-safe container, and then scatter the ashes.

The second option is especially good if the knots you have named have been with you for a long time. Hold on to the thread and, in the amount of time that feels right to you, consider each knot in turn, working with it, unraveling it mentally, emotionally, and spiritually, and then actually untying it. Once you have untied all of the knots, you may hang the thread in a tree so that birds, squirrels, or other critters can take it and create their homes with it, transforming it into blessing material.

However you decide to conclude the ceremony, end with the following or something like it: "Amen/Thank you/ So it is/It is done."

Breathe in a blessing on the work you have done. Exhale in gratitude.

STEPPING STONES

- Often textiles are decorated with symbols that have ancient meanings. Common motifs include birds, bells, flowers, diamond patterns, and spirals. Look at your own clothes, especially the pieces that you love to wear, and notice what symbols, if any, adorn them. What do those symbols mean to you?

- Make an offering to your blessed body and engage in some thread magic by procuring one article of clothing that you really love. You can buy it, trade for it, happen across it in a thrift store. Present it to yourself like the gift that it is.

- Pick out a shawl or light blanket and dedicate it as your prayer shawl. Wear it whenever you engage in any magical work and notice how it makes you feel when you wear it versus when you do not.

Making Magic has charted a path between two points: it begins with seeking and is fulfilled in a certain realization. Seeking the wild creature that is magic, within the lands and the woods of the soul, leads to the understanding that all along this wild creature has also been seeking, shadowing, and stalking us, lying in wait for us, waiting for us to return. We move from seeking magic to finding it, from remembering it to making it, and as the worlds are woven together, living it.

A journey, a pilgrimage, a wandering, a wondering, and yes, a weaving of remembered magic has taken place. Woven back together are the elements of self and soul; woven back together are all that we encounter every day and the extraordinary that lives right inside of it. Woven back together are the elements of every broken place. With each step we have taken, every commitment we have kept close, every adventure in sacred imagination we have undergone, and even the smallest ritual we have practiced, we have completed the most vital work of restoration: that of calling forth the blessings. May we, the world we inhabit, and the world we pass on to those who come after us be healed, made whole, and be seen as deeply holy once more. This is the true power of magic.

POSTLUDE

Somewhere in the world right now you are remembering your very own wild magic. Striding alongside it, you will find that you have discovered a set of instructions after all. They will guide you in creating rituals, fostering transformation, coming into right relationship with your uncharted soul soil, seeing what has up until this point remained unseen, hearing what has up until this point remained unheard, and giving voice to that which has been voiceless. They are the signposts for making magic.

Dream true.
Listen to your dreams.
Ask a question.
Seek an answer.
Be purposeful.
Bring an offering.
Discern with care who is worth listening to.
Go into the wild.
Show kindness to strangers.
Accept that the journey will take as much time as it takes.
Do not rush.
Do not dawdle.
Pay attention.
Find the cave.
Ford the river.
Be willing to wait for what is worthwhile.
Sit by the fire.

Make it your own.
Stay as long as it takes.
Laugh.
Love.
Tell stories.
Say thank you.
Know your true name.
Remember what matters.
Live life so that others can remember too.
Dare to speak to bears.

ACKNOWLEDGMENTS

In my own life, it would be difficult to say who did the seeking. Did I seek out the wild animal that is magic, or did it seek me out, claiming me as its own and rubbing its scent all over me from a very early age? Many of us feel this way, and it is what makes soulful seeking the never-ending dance that it is. What I do know is that I am privileged to be born into a family of fantastic people who tell wonderful stories and live colorful lives. It is from them that I have learned in a thousand small and significant ways how to spy the golden threads of the extraordinary right in the middle of all that is everyday.

Making magic is always a community effort, and the same is true about writing a book. Though my name is on the cover, the truth is that the book you hold in your hands has an entire flock of holy helpers who taught me, challenged me, supported me, and fed me in body, soul, and spirit. In writing their names down here, I honor, bless, and thank each and every one of them.

The deepest and brightest thank you goes to my beloved husband, David—first editor, sounding board, and man who brings coffee, beauty, and loving touches, as well as a sharp mind and deep heart. This work is as much yours as mine. You are my beloved, and I am blessed beyond measure by your presence in my life.

Greatest thanks to my earliest teachers, my parents, Bill and Brenda, each of whom taught me their own unique mix of alchemy, magic, and wonder. My Nana, who teaches me daily about the power of prayer, among so many other things, and my Papa, for being the first bringer of magic in my life and teaching me a valuable lesson early on—that people really can change. My sister, Brittany, for agreeing all those years ago to be a little witch right alongside me. My Uncle Bubba taught me early on what it meant to go your own way and what hunting for food is really all about. My extended family, all of whom circle around the bonfire at the beach—you are home base and tribe, and I feel each of you with me on this journey.

Ideas have their own lineages that are passed down hand to hand and voice to voice by excellent teachers. Some of mine have been Chris Parma, Matthew Davis, Chester Burke, Deborah Schwartz, Patricia Greer, Flora Elmore, Myra Krien, catherine yronwode, Natalie Goldberg, Dr. Clarissa Pinkola Estés, R. J. Stewart, and Anastacia Nutt, among so many others. Terri Windling deserves deep thanks for sharing my writing with her audience and encouraging my voice at a critical time, as well as for her own fantastic literary work, which continues to be a source of inspiration and wonder. Midori Snyder deserves thanks for consistently crafting beautiful words and being an exemplar of the art.

Friendship has also been an essential magical ingredient along this journey, so I must thank my best friend Roxana Zirakzadeh for being the best friend anyone could ask for, a sister, cheerleader, and fellow philosopher and lover of beauty all rolled into one perfect package. I would also like to thank the following companions who have walked many miles with me: Colleen Buckley, Jon De Los Santos, Marion Cook, Dr. Felicia Stonedale (a real-life fairy godmother), Heather Hunter (*tía* extraordinaire), Leslie Wolfe, Paul and James Chapman, Wendy and Randall Cherry, my parent crew at San Antonio Academy, and the countless friends I have made online who are far too numerous to name. I have been blessed with not only dear friends but also dear colleagues. Special thanks to Theresa Reed for opening the door, the road, and the way and for being the best. Danielle Cohen is my photographer and witness in so many ways. Thanks also to Fabeku Fatunmise, Jason Miller, Aidan Wachter, Elizabeth Barrial, Esmé Wang, Alexis Morgan, Jen Holmes, Sara Magnuson, Jacquelyn Tierney, Anais, Shannon, and Abby.

A deep bow goes out to my students, clients, and community of soulful seekers, many of whom have been with me year in and year out. I love you all and am honored to serve you. And another deep bow to my team: Monica Mitchell, who keeps the tech aspects of my site up and running, and Cassandra Oswald, who has become a collaborative partner and provides all of the original art on the site, as well as for the cover of this book. Thanks to Sounds True. Jennifer Brown is not just an acquisitions editor; she is a true friend and advocate. To my editor, Amy Rost, who understood me and my vision from day one. And to Tami Simon, who kept looking at my work and giving it a chance.

Thanks and best of blessings to my sons. To Jasper, my first business partner, discerning client, and one of the goads to begin teaching. And thanks of another kind to Heath, with whom I was pregnant throughout the entire crafting of this book and who in a very real way wrote this book with me. You are both my joys and miracles.

I thank the crossroads and all they have taught me, and the daily reminder to call out the magic.

Final thanks are given to my ancestors, those who came before me and whose voices were often muted, muzzled, and for far too long went unheard, and to my descendants, those who will come after I am gone. My prayer for you is that you inherit a world more mended and magical.

NOTES

EPIGRAPH

William Wordsworth, "Lines Composed a Few Miles Above Tintern Abbey, on Revisiting the Banks of the Wye During a Tour. July 13, 1798," *The Oxford Book of Nineteenth Century English Verse*, ed. John Hayward (London: Oxford University Press, 1964), 66.

CHAPTER 1: REMEMBER YOUR MAGIC

1. Eden Phillpotts, *A Shadow Passes* (London: C. Palmer & Hayward, 1918), 19.
2. Claude Lévi-Strauss, *Tristes Tropiques*, trans. John and Doreen Weightman (New York: Modern Library, 1997), 29.
3. René Descartes, *Discourse on Method and Meditations on First Philosophy*, trans. Donald A. Cress (Indianapolis: Hackett, 1998), 59.

CHAPTER 2: MEMORY AND IMAGINATION

1. Hesiod, "Theogony," *The Homeric Hymns and Homerica*, trans. Hugh G. Evelyn-White (Cambridge, MA; Harvard University Press; London: William Heinemann, 1914), line 60. Available online at perseus.tufts.edu/hopper/text?doc=Perseus%3Atext%3A1999.01 .0130%3Acard%3D53.
2. Elizabeth G. Vermilyea, *Growing Beyond Survival: A Self-Help Toolkit for Managing Traumatic Stress*, 2nd ed. (Brooklandville, MD: Sidran Press, 2013).

CHAPTER 3: FINDING THE DOORS

1. William Blake, *The Marriage of Heaven and Hell* (London: William Blake, 1790). Illuminated book viewable online via the William Blake Archive (blakearchive.org). This quote is found on object 14 of 27 (Bentley 14, Erdman 14, Keynes 14), blakearchive.org /copy/mhh.a?descId=mhh.a.illbk.14. The original book is held at Houghton Library, Harvard University, Cambridge, MA.

CHAPTER 4: TREASURES AND TOUCHSTONES

1. Dōgen, "Fukanzazengi 普勧坐禅儀 (Universal Promotion of the Principles of Zazen)," *The Heart of Dōgen's Shōbōgenzō*, trans. Norman Waddell and Masao Abe (New York: SUNY Press, 2002), 2.
2. Matthew 6:21 (New International Version).
3. Dōgen, "Genjōkōan 現成公按 (Manifesting Suchness)," *The Heart of Dōgen's Shōbōgenzō*, trans. Norman Waddell and Masao Abe (New York: SUNY Press, 2002), 42. Original context: "Man does not obstruct enlightenment any more than the drop of dew obstructs the moon or the heavens. The depth of one will be the measure of the other's height."
4. Ióannés Stobaios, *Anthologium III*, ed. C. Wachsmuth and O. Hense (Berlin: Apud Weidmannos, 1894), 173. "Know thyself" translates γνῶθι σαυτόν, and "None too much," μηδὲν ἄγαν. These are but two of 147 known maxims attributed to the Oracle at Delphi.

CHAPTER 5: TAKING YOUR TIME

1. William Shakespeare, "Venus and Adonis," *The Complete Works of William Shakespeare*, ed. W. J. Craig (London: Oxford University Press, 1947), 1075, lines 129–30.
2. C. S. Lewis, *The Lion, the Witch, and the Wardrobe*, illus. Pauline Baynes (New York: HarperCollins, 2008), 82.

CHAPTER 6: KITH AND KIN

1. Linda Hogan, *Dwellings: A Spiritual History of the Living World* (New York: Norton, 1995), 159.
2. *Plato's Symposium*, trans. Seth Benardete (Chicago: University of Chicago Press, 2001), 22.

CHAPTER 7: KNOWING NATURE

1. George Eliot, *Middlemarch* (New York: Barnes and Noble Classics, 2003), 185.

CHAPTER 8: HEARTH AND HOME

1. Annie Dillard, *Holy the Firm* (New York: Harper & Row, 1977), 62.

CHAPTER 9: CALL AND RESPONSE

1. Carl Jung, *The Red Book: A Reader's Edition*, ed. Sonu Shamdasani, trans. John Peck and Mark Kyburz (New York: W. W. Norton, 2012), 132.
2. Carl Jung, *Synchronicity: An Acausal Connecting Principle*, trans. R. F. C. Hull (Princeton, NJ: Princeton University Press, 2010).
3. Sigmund Freud, *The Interpretation of Dreams*, trans. A. A. Brill (New York: Modern Library, 1994). See in particular chapter 2, "The Method of Dream Interpretation," 9–12.

CHAPTER 10: PRAYING DOWN HARD

1. Hank Williams, vocalist, "Thank God," hymn written by Fred Rose, MGM Records, 1955.
2. Thomas Merton, *No Man Is an Island* (Boston: Shambhala Publications, 2005), xiii.
3. Rumi, "The Great Wagon," *The Essential Rumi*, trans. Coleman Barks, with John Moyne (New York: Harper Collins, 1995), 35.

CHAPTER 11: WATERS AND WASHING

1. Kenneth Clark, *Leonardo da Vinci,* rev. ed. (New York: Penguin, 1989), 38.

CHAPTER 12: HOLDING SPACE

1. Laozi (Lao-tzu), *Taoteching*, trans. Red Pine (Bill Porter) (San Francisco: Mercury House, 1996), 22.

CHAPTER 13: SMOKE AND FIRE

1. Dante Alighieri, "Paradiso," *The Divine Comedy*, vol. 3, trans. Charles S. Singleton (Princeton, NJ: Princeton University Press, 1975), 5.
2. Ursula K. Le Guin, *A Wizard of Earthsea (The Earthsea Cycle)* (New York: Houghton Mifflin, 2012), 57.
3. "Rabbit Boy," *American Indian Myths and Legends*, ed. Richard Erdoes and Alfonso Ortiz (New York: Pantheon Books, 1984), 5–8.
4. *The Rig Veda*, trans. Wendy Doniger (New York: Penguin, 1981), 99–117.

5. For an interesting discussion of the ancient Greek and Roman attitudes toward sacred fire, review chapter 3, "Sacred Fire," in Numa Denis Fustel de Coulanges, *The Ancient City: A Study in the Religion, Laws, and Institutions of Greek and Rome* (Baltimore: John's Hopkins University Press, 1980), 17–25.

CHAPTER 14: WEAVING THE WORLDS BACK TOGETHER

1. Rebecca Solnit, *The Faraway Nearby* (New York: Penguin, 2014), 130.

SUGGESTED READING

Abram, David. *Becoming Animal: An Earthly Cosmology.* New York: Vintage Classics, 2010.

Aland, Barbara, Kurt Aland, Johannes Karavidopoulos, Carlo M. Martini, and Bruce Metzger, eds. *The Greek New Testament.* Germany: United Bible Societies, 1998.

Andrews, Tamra. *Nectar and Ambrosia: An Encyclopedia of Food in World Mythology.* Santa Barbara: ABC-CLIO, 2000.

Berk, Ari, and Carolyn Dunn. *Coyote Speaks: Wonders of the Native American World.* New York: Abrams Books for Young Readers, 2008.

Berry, Wendell. *Sex, Economy, Freedom & Community: Eight Essays.* New York: Pantheon, 1993.

Bettelheim, Bruno. *The Uses of Enchantment: The Meaning and Importance of Fairy Tales.* New York: Vintage Classics, 2010.

Bloch, Ariel, and Chana Bloch, trans. *The Song of Songs: A New Translation with an Introduction and Commentary.* Berkeley: University of California Press, 1998.

Carr-Gomm, Philip, and Richard Heygate. *The Book of English Magic.* London: John Murray, 2010.

Coffman, Sam. *The Herbal Medic.* Vol. 1. San Antonio: The Human Path, 2014.

Connelly, Joan Breton. *The Parthenon Enigma.* New York: Vintage, 2014.

de Coulanges, Numa Denis Fustel. *The Ancient City: A Study on the Religion, Laws, and Institutions of Greece and Rome.* Baltimore: Johns Hopkins University Press, 1980.

Datlow, Ellen, and Terri Windling, eds. *The Coyote Road: Trickster Tales.* New York: Firebird (Penguin), 2007.

Dōgen. *The Heart of Dōgen's Shobogenzo.* Translated by Norman Waddell and Masao Abe. New York: SUNY Press, 2002.

Doniger, Wendy, trans. *The Rig Veda.* New York: Penguin Books, 1981.

Eliade, Mircea. *The Sacred and the Profane: The Nature of Religion.* Translated by Willard R. Trask. New York: Harcourt, 1987.

Erdoes, Richard, and Alfonso Ortiz, eds. *American Indian Myths and Legends.* New York: Pantheon Books, 1984.

Estés, Clarissa Pinkola. *Women Who Run with the Wolves: Myths and Stories of the Wild Woman Archetype.* New York: Ballantine, 1992.

Frazer, George James. *The Golden Bough: A Study of Magic and Religion.* New York: Simon and Schuster, 1996.

Froud, Brian, and Alan Lee. *Faeries.* New York: Harry N. Abrams, 1978.

Gary, Gemma. *Wisht Waters: Aqueous Magica and the Cult of Holy Wells.* Richmond Vista, CA: Three Hands Press, 2014.

Ginzburg, Carlo. *Ecstasies: Deciphering the Witches' Sabbath.* Translated by Raymond Rosenthal. Chicago: University of Chicago Press, 2004.

Graf, Fritz. *Magic in the Ancient World.* Translated by Franklin Philip. Cambridge, MA: Harvard University Press, 1999.

Hogan, Linda. *Dwellings: A Spiritual History of the Living World.* New York: Norton, 1995.

Joyce, Graham. *The Limits of Enchantment: A Novel.* New York: Washington Square Press, 2005.

Kimmerer, Robin Wall. *Braiding Sweetgrass: Indigenous Wisdom, Scientific Knowledge, and the Teaching of Plants.* Minneapolis: Milkweed Editions, 2013.

Laozi. *Taoteching.* Translated by Red Pine. San Francisco: Mercury House, 1996.

Latorre, Dolores. *Cooking and Curing with Mexican Herbs.* Austin: The Encino Press, 1977.

Lecouteux, Claude. *The High Magic of Talismans and Amulets: Tradition and Craft.* Rochester, VT: Inner Traditions, 2005.

Lévy, Isaac Jack, and Rosemary Lévy Zumwalt. *Ritual Medical Lore of Sephardic Women: Sweetening the Spirits, Healing the Sick.* Champaign: University of Illinois Press, 2002.

Lopez, Barry. *Vintage Lopez*. New York: Vintage, 2004.

MacFarlane, Robert. *The Wild Places*. New York: Penguin Books, 2008.

Maitland, Sara. *Gossip from the Forest: The Tangled Roots of Our Forests and Fairytales*. London: Granta Publications, 2013.

Moore, Kathleen Dean. *Wild Comfort: The Solace of Nature*. Boulder, CO: Trumpeter, 2010.

Müller-Ebeling, Claudia, Christian Ratsch, and Wolf-Dieter Storl. *Witchcraft Medicine: Healing Arts, Shamanic Practices, and Forbidden Plants*. Translated by Annabel Lee. Rochester, VT: Inner Traditions, 1998.

Nabhan, Gary Paul. *The Desert Smells Like Rain: A Naturalist in O'odham Country*. Tucson: The University of Arizona Press, 2002.

Plotinus. *The Essential Plotinus*. Translated by Elmer O'Brien. Indianapolis: Hackett Publishing, 1964.

Purkiss, Diane. *At the Bottom of the Garden: A Dark History of Fairies, Hobgoblins, Nymphs, and Other Troublesome Things*. New York: New York University Press, 2003.

Raine, Kathleen, and George Mills Harper, eds. *Thomas Taylor the Platonist: Selected Writings*. Princeton, NJ: Princeton University Press, 1969.

Reed, Theresa. *The Tarot Coloring Book*. Boulder, CO: Sounds True, 2016.

Roth, Harold. *The Witching Herbs: 13 Essential Plants and Herbs for Your Magical Garden*. Boston: Weiser Books, 2017.

Scheindlin, Raymond P., trans. *The Book of Job*. New York: W. W. Norton, 1998.

Shakespeare, William. *The Complete Works of William Shakespeare*. Edited by W. J. Craig. London: Oxford University Press, 1947.

Silko, Leslie Marmon. *Ceremony*. New York: Viking Press, 1977.

Stuckey, Priscilla. *Kissed by a Fox: And Other Stories of Friendship in Nature*. Berkeley, CA: Counterpoint Press, 2012.

Tanakh: The Holy Scriptures. Philadelphia: The Jewish Publication Society, 1985.

Tatar, Maria, ed. *The Annotated Classic Fairy Tales*. New York: W. W. Norton, 2002.

Thomas, Keith. *Religion and the Decline of Magic: Studies in Popular Beliefs in Sixteenth- and Seventeenth-Century England*. New York: Penguin, 1971.

Tolkien, J.R.R. *The Monsters and the Critics: And Other Essays*. London: Harper Collins, 1983.

Virgil. *The Aeneid*. Translated by Robert Fitzgerald. New York: Vintage Books, 1990.

Wachter, Aidan. *Six Ways: Approaches & Entries for Practical Magic*. Albuquerque, NM: Red Temple Press, 2018.

Walker, Barbara G. *The Women's Encyclopedia of Myths and Secrets*. New York: HarperCollins, 1983.

Warner, Marina. *From the Beast to the Blonde: On Fairy Tales and Their Tellers*. New York: Farrar, Straus, and Giroux, 1994.

Wilby, Emma. *Cunning Folk and Familiar Spirits: Shamanistic Visionary Traditions in Early Modern British Witchcraft and Magic*. Brighton, UK: Sussex Academic Press, 2005.

Windling, Terri. *The Wood Wife*. New York: Tor Books. 1996.

Yates, Francis. *The Art of Memory*. Chicago: University of Chicago Press, 1966.

Yolen, Jane. *Touch Magic: Fantasy, Faerie, and Folklore in the Literature of Childhood*. Atlanta, GA: August House, 2000.

Yronwode, Catherine. *Hoodoo Herb and Root Magic: A Materia Magica of African-American Conjure*. Forestville, CA: Lucky Mojo Curio Company, 2002.

Yronwode, Catherine. *Hoodoo Rootwork Correspondence Course*. Forestville, CA: Lucky Mojo Curio Company, 2006.

Zipes, Jack, ed. *The Original Folk and Fairy Tales of the Brothers Grimm: The Complete First Edition*. Princeton, NJ: Princeton University Press, 2014.

ABOUT THE AUTHOR

Briana Saussy is a writer, teacher, spiritual counselor, and ritualist dedicated to the restoration and remembering of the sacred arts. She combines a practical and creative approach to spirituality that includes the riches of the perennial world religions, the contributions of modern psychology to the search for meaning, and the often overlooked and forgotten bodies of wisdom contained in folk magic, divination, and storytelling practices. Briana studied Eastern and Western classics, philosophy, mathematics, and science at St. John's College (Annapolis and Santa Fe) and is a student of Ancient Greek and Sanskrit.

Briana comes from a diverse lineage of South Texans whose ethnic heritage includes Scotch-Irish, Cherokee, Chickasaw, Mexican, and Jewish roots, and who have informed her own direct experience with survivals of fragmented folk magic and storytelling traditions. She lives in her hometown of San Antonio, Texas, with her husband and two sons, as well as various furred, finned, and feathered friends. Beyond conversations that make her think, sweet kisses from her beloved, and good times with her family, she finds that strong coffee, good dirt, and true words are some of the best things in life. You may learn more about her work at brianasaussy.com.

ABOUT SOUNDS TRUE

Sounds True is a multimedia publisher whose mission is to inspire and support personal transformation and spiritual awakening. Founded in 1985 and located in Boulder, Colorado, we work with many of the leading spiritual teachers, thinkers, healers, and visionary artists of our time. We strive with every title to preserve the essential "living wisdom" of the author or artist. It is our goal to create products that not only provide information to a reader or listener, but that also embody the quality of a wisdom transmission.

For those seeking genuine transformation, Sounds True is your trusted partner. At SoundsTrue.com you will find a wealth of free resources to support your journey, including exclusive weekly audio interviews, free downloads, interactive learning tools, and other special savings on all our titles.

To learn more, please visit SoundsTrue.com/freegifts or call us toll-free at 800.333.9185.